THE HOLISTIC CURRICULUM
Second Edition

Holistic education is concerned with connections in human experience: connections between mind and body, between linear and intuitive ways of knowing, between individual and community, and between the personal self and the transpersonal self.

First published in 1988, *The Holistic Curriculum* examines the philosophical, psychological, and social foundations of holistic education, outlining its history and discussing practical applications in the classroom.

This revised and expanded second edition concisely describes how holistic thinking integrates spiritual and scientific perspectives, and draws on romantic, humanistic, and other radical alternatives to the atomistic worldview of the modern age. The role of the teacher, the issue of accountability, and strategies for implementing the holistic curriculum are also discussed.

JOHN P. MILLER is a professor in the Centre for Teacher Development at the Ontario Institute for Studies in Education of the University of Toronto.

JOHN P. MILLER

The Holistic Curriculum

Second Edition

OISE Press

Since 1901

University of Toronto Press
Toronto Buffalo London

Printed in Canada

First published in 1988 by OISE Press Inc., Toronto, Canada; revised and expanded edition published in 1996 by OISE Press; reprinted 2001.

Reprinted 2008

ISBN 978-0-8020-9218-2 (cloth)
ISBN 978-0-8020-9449-0 (paper)

∞

Printed on acid-free paper

Library and Archives Canada Cataloguing in Publication

Miller, John P., 1943–
The holistic curriculum / John P. Miller. – 2nd ed.

Includes bibliographical references and index.
ISBN 978-0-8020-9218-2 (bound)
ISBN 978-0-8020-9449-0 (pbk.)

1. Education – Philosophy. 2. Education – Curricula. 3. Curriculum planning. I. Ontario Institute for Studies in Education II. Title.

LB1025.2.M44 2007   370.1   C2006-907047-4

The University of Toronto Press acknowledges the financial assistance to its publishing program of the Canada Council for the Arts and the Ontario Arts Council.

University of Toronto Press acknowledges the financial support for its publishing activities of the Government of Canada through the Book Publishing Industry Development Program (BPIDP).

Contents

Preface

The first edition of this book was published in 1988. That was also the year when Ron Miller began publishing the *Holistic Education Review*, which was eventually renamed *Encounter*. The Global Alliance for Transforming Education was formed and meetings were held around North America to explore various approaches to holistic education. The late 1980s and early 1990s were encouraging times for holistic education. We now live in a period when educators are more interested in testing students than exploring how they can learn and develop as human beings. Repeatedly we hear the mantra that education must prepare students so that they can compete in the global economy. Despite this climate, interest in holistic education has been expanding around the world. For example, this book has been translated into Japanese and Korean and currently is being translated into Chinese. I have been privileged to participate in conferences around the world hosted by holistic educators who have initiated grassroots movements in their own countries. These activities, which include conferences, formation of holistic education societies, and the founding of schools with a holistic focus, exist on every continent. Since the late 1990s the closely related field of spirituality in education has grown, and several books on the topic have been published, such as Rachael Kessler's *Soul in Education* and Parker Palmer's *Courage to Teach*.

In this second revision of *The Holistic Curriculum* I have attempted to address the issue of accountability from a holistic perspective as well as other issues that have arisen in the past decade. I have also expanded Chapter 5 on the history of holistic education as I continued to read and learn more about how our ancestors approached teaching and learning holistically. Finally, I have attempted to include updated examples of holistic education practices.

I am very grateful to the many students I have worked with at my own institution, the Ontario Institute for Studies in Education at the University of Toronto, and at Kobe Shinwa Women's University and Ritsumeikan University in Japan. Their insights and enthusiasm continually renew and inspire me. Thanks particularly to Karen Csoli, a doctoral student at OISE/UT, for helping me with the research and editing of this book. I am also very grateful to Stephen Kotowych and Bill Harnum at the University of Toronto Press for supporting and encouraging me to do this revision. Thanks also to Jim Leahy, who so carefully copy-edited the manuscript.

John P. Miller

PART ONE

Holistic Curriculum:
The Context

CHAPTER ONE

Holistic Curriculum: The Why and the What

Holistic education attempts to bring education into alignment with the fundamental realities of nature. Nature at its core is interrelated and dynamic. We can see this dynamism and connectedness in the atom, organic systems, the biosphere, and the universe itself (Capra 1996). Unfortunately, the human world since the Industrial Revolution has stressed compartmentalization and standardization. The result has been fragmentation.

This fragmentation permeates everything (Senge, Scharmer, Jaworski & Flowers, 2005, p. 190). First, we have separated economic life from the surrounding environment, and the result has been ecological devastation. The air we breathe and the water we drink are often foul. We seem to have poisoned everything, including the vast expanses of the oceans, because we see ourselves as separate from the organic processes that surround us.

A second kind of fragmentation is social fragmentation. Most people in industrialized societies live in large cities, where they feel afraid and cut off from others. Although crime rates have dropped over the past decade, violence in urban areas is still a concern in North American cities. People are afraid to walk alone at night even in areas that used to be considered 'safe,' such as the suburbs. The fragmentation can also be seen in the various forms of abuse that we witness today. We abuse ourselves with tobacco, alcohol, and drugs. We abuse others including the elderly, spouses, and children. This abuse, I believe, arises when people feel unconnected to each other and cut off from valid forms of community.

Another form of fragmentation is within ourselves. Emerson (1990) wrote, 'The reason why the world lacks unity, and lies broken and in

heaps, is because man is disunited with himself' (p. 54). We find ourselves disconnected from our bodies and our hearts. Education specifi-
cally has done much to sever the relationship between head and heart.
Anything that is not part of academic discourse is labelled 'touchy-
feely.' As a result, in industrialized society we live in our heads, denying our deeper knowing and intuitions.

Finally, Joseph Campbell (1986) has described another form of fragmentation in our culture – a lack of shared sense of meaning, or mythology. In North America there seem to be no shared values; the media
constantly refer to the cultural wars in the United States. This lack of
consensus becomes apparent when we try to deal with such issues as
gun control, abortion, euthanasia, and gay rights. The closest we come
to a worldview is scientific materialism, which is exemplified by the
media and the education system. This worldview suggests that the only
reality is physical and that the only way we can understand and control
this reality is through the scientific method. Materialism is connected to
consumerism, which encourages us to collect as many material goods
as possible. The more goods we have, the better we are supposed to
feel. However, many people who have acquired material well-being do
not feel whole. Gregg Easterbrook (2003) documents how people today
live much better materially than their parents and grandparents but are
not as happy. Some people sense something is missing and, for the lack
of a better word, we call this something 'spirituality.' Here we define
spirituality as a sense of the awe and reverence for life that arises from
our relatedness to something both wonderful and mysterious.

The fragmentation I have been describing is also found in our education system. We divide knowledge into subjects, units, and lessons.
Yet students can often not see the relationship between these subjects,
the relationship between facts within a subject, or the relevance of the
subject to their own lives. The Batesons (1987) have summarized this
point:

> The truth that the aborigine and the peasant share is the truth of integra-
> tion. By contrast, we must be concerned today because, although we can
> persuade our children to learn a long list of facts about the world, they
> don't seem to have the capacity to put them together in a single, unified
> understanding – there is no 'pattern that connects.' (p. 196)

It is clear that we live in a time of transition. The old industrial order is crumbling. Large hierarchical organizations from the communist

state to large, unresponsive organizations such as General Motors are imploding or 'radically restructuring' themselves to survive. The factory model is dying. Yet we are not sure what is replacing it. However, it is possible to identify certain images that reflect a new, emerging mythology. One image that has been cited by Joseph Campbell and others is the picture of the earth taken from the moon. This picture has enhanced a sense of global connectedness as it shows a world without boundaries. Russell Schwiekart, a U.S. astronaut said, 'You look down there and you can't imagine how many borders and boundaries you crossed again and again and again. And you don't even see 'em ... From where you see it, the thing is a whole, and it's so beautiful' (as cited in Senge, 1990, p. 370).

Looking at that picture can restore in us a sense of awe and wonder. In the nineteenth century, Emerson suggested that human beings had lost their 'original relation to universe' (1990, p. 25). If this was true in that century, it is even more poignant today as the media have become our lens to the universe. One of the reasons for the renewed interest in indigenous people's spirituality is that their worldview has helped awaken in us our original relationship to nature.

Another important image is the fall of the Berlin wall. This event represented both the end of the cold war and the metaphorical collapse of other walls. For example, for centuries people of different racial background, sexual orientation, or ability have been excluded, institutionalized, or discriminated against. Now people are demanding to be treated as human beings. We still have a long way to go in dealing with these issues, but at least now they have become part of our consciousness and legislation has done much to begin the process of building a more inclusive society.

The images of the earth and the coming down of the Berlin wall support a new mythology based on a sense of interdependence and connection. Rooted in the reality of nature itself and supported by various spiritual traditions, this vision of interdependence is at the heart of many changes in business, health, and education. The impetus behind the change is to put our life and our institutions more in harmony with the way things are. If nature is dynamic and interconnected and our education system is static and fragmented, then we only promote alienation and suffering. But if we can align the institutions with this interconnection and dynamism, then the possibilities for human fulfillment increase greatly.

People often ask about the root meaning of 'holistic.' The word 'holistic' comes from the Greek word 'holon' and refers to a universe made up of integrated wholes that cannot simply be reduced to the sum of its parts. Holistic is sometimes spelled as 'wholistic.' I do not use the words interchangeably, but suggest that 'holistic' implies spirituality, or a sense of the sacred, while 'wholistic' is more material and biological with an emphasis on physical and social interconnections. I believe Dewey argued for wholism, while Gandhi and Steiner were holistic in their perspectives.

Holistic Education: Balance, Inclusion, and Connection

Holistic education is founded on three basic principles: balance, inclusion, and connection.

Balance

The philosophical roots for balance come from the Tao and the concepts of *yin* and *yang*, which are seen as complementary and interconnected energies. Yin and yang each contain the seed of the other, and thus

Figure 1.1 Yin and Yang

each is transforming into the other. Laurence Boldt (1999) describes the relationship between the two: 'All things have arisen mutually and mutually supportive, in the sense that they require one another as a condition of their existence. The man requires the woman; the woman, the man; the night requires the day; the day the night; the good, the bad; the bad, the good and so on' (p. 27). The symbol for yin and yang is well known (fig. 1.1).

The yin and yang need each other for there to be health in the cosmos, the earth, cultures, institutions (e.g., schools and classrooms), and the individual. If one predominates to the exclusion of the other, sickness arises. One could argue that Western culture and education have been dominated by the yang, which tends to emphasize the rational, the material, the masculine, and the individual to the exclusion of the intuitive, the spiritual, the feminine, and the group. This imbalance, one could argue, has led to sickness in cultures and institutions.

Let us look at the classroom in terms of yin and yang:

Yin	Yang
Group	Individual
Process	Content
Imagination	Knowledge
Intuitive	Rational
Qualitative assessment	Quantitative assessment
Instruction/learning	Assessment/evaluation
Program	Technology
Vision	Techniques/strategies

INDIVIDUAL/GROUP

Education in North America has tended to emphasize individual competition rather than group collaboration. Although this has changed somewhat with greater emphasis being placed on cooperative learning, the current focus on testing and individual achievement strongly reinforces the yang energy in the classroom. Students compete against each other on standardized tests in order to move through the system.

CONTENT/PROCESS

Covering content has often been at the centre of the curriculum and teaching. However, with the knowledge explosion and a rapidly changing world, there has been interest in helping students to learn and to process information.

KNOWLEDGE/IMAGINATION

Curriculum reformers such as Hirsch, Kett, and Trefil (1988) have argued that children should learn certain essential knowledge, and this should take priority in teaching. Another view is that knowledge is co-created as students construct their own meaning and ways of knowing. Imagination plays an important role in this process. Recent curriculum reforms, however, have tended to emphasize content and testing how well students have covered the content.

RATIONAL/INTUITIVE

Our education system and the culture as a whole have emphasized rational and linear approaches to problems. A more holistic approach calls for a merging of reason and intuition. When these two elements are connected, student thinking is enriched. However, approaches that emphasize intuition rarely seem to enter the classroom. Although human beings have used techniques such as imagery work for centuries (Samuels & Samuels, 1975), they are identified as too 'new age' and thus are often excluded from teaching.

QUANTITATIVE/QUALITATIVE ASSESSMENT

Quantitative assessment is represented by the standardized test, which tends to dominate in the age of accountability. Qualitative assessment is seen in the use of portfolios, where a continuum of student work can be seen and assessed. Portfolios and other forms of qualitative assessment have made inroads but students and teachers in elementary schools in the United States have focused on the quantitative testing associated with programs such as No Child Left Behind.

TECHNIQUE/VISION

In the West we have tended to focus on technique. In education this has meant an excessive emphasis on teaching and assessment strategies without a corresponding link to a broader conception of learning and a vision of the whole child. In contrast, educators such as Maria Montessori and Rudolf Steiner offer a balance between technique and a vision of the whole person.

ASSESSMENT/LEARNING

Today we seem almost obsessed with testing and reporting. When this obsession becomes strong we tend to lose our focus on learning, particularly natural, organic learning processes. Curriculum becomes teaching to the test rather than facilitating learning. A balance needs to be restored between assessment and learning. Anne Quindlen (2005), a commentator for *Newsweek* magazine, has written: 'Our education system is broken; accountability and standards will fix it. This is the mantra of government testing programs, from local certifications to the federal No Child Left Behind program, which might as well be called No Child Left Untested' (p. 88).

TECHNOLOGY/PROGRAM

Another current obsession is technology. Some educators argue that a computer is needed for every child in the classroom. Again, a broader programmatic vision is important to set technology in a proper context. A technology-driven curriculum is ultimately a narrow and limited curriculum.

Holistic teaching seeks a balance between the whole and the part. Generally, we have focused on the part as we have broken the curriculum into subjects, units, and lessons. Yet we lack an encompassing vision that inspires us. In the holistic curriculum we attempt to link the unit and lesson to a larger vision. This vision can vary but it usually involves a sense of interdependence and personal wholeness. Tolle (2005) describes his vision of the whole:

> One the one hand, the whole comprises all that exists. It is the world or the cosmos. But all things in existence, from microbes to human beings to galaxies, are not really separate things or entities, but form part of a web of interconnected multidimensional processes. (p. 276)

The Roman emperor Marcus Aurelius (1997) also presented a vision of the relationship between the individual and the whole:

> Whether the universe is a concourse of atoms, or nature is a system, let this first be established: that I am a part of the whole that is governed by nature; next, that I stand in some intimate connection with other kindred parts. For remembering this, inasmuch as I am a part, I shall be discontented with none of the things that are assigned to me out of the whole; for nothing is injurious to the part if it's for the advantage of the whole. (p. 77)

The holistic curriculum then seeks the 'right relationship' between the part and the whole where both are acknowledged and nourished.

Inclusiveness

Another way to look at holistic education is to link together various educational orientations. This section describes three orientations – transmission, transaction, and transformation – and considers how they might be viewed in a holistic manner (Miller & Seller, 1985).

TRANSMISSION POSITION

In transmission learning the student acquires and accumulates knowledge and skills. Learning in this form can occur by reading a text or listening to a teacher's explanation. Knowledge is seen as fixed rather than as a process, and is usually broken down into smaller units so that students can master the material. Transmission learning is common when we begin to learn a particular skill. For example, in order to drive we have to learn the basic rules of driving, and thus we study the driving handbook so we can pass the written test.

In learning to perform a skill, transmission learning tends to be imitative and repetitive. The young child learns to talk by imitating the speech of his or her parents. In learning a sports skill, such as hitting a golf ball, we watch the instructor and then repeat the skill over and over.

The transmission position has a long history and consists of two strands. One strand is the behavioural; the second strand focuses on the standard subjects taught in a traditional style (for example, lecture and recitation). In either case the relationship between the curriculum and child is illustrated in figure 1.2.

Figure 1.2 Transmission Position

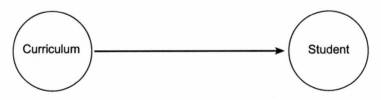

In the behavioural strand this relationship is known as stimulus-response (S-R), while in the traditional subject curriculum the teacher or text conveys information to the student. In both cases there is a one-way flow, or transmission, of skills and knowledge. There is little or no opportunity to reflect on or analyse the information.

TRANSACTION POSITION

Transactional learning is more interactive, although the interaction is mainly cognitive. In transaction learning, the student must often solve a problem or pursue some form of inquiry. Knowledge is not viewed as something that is fixed in small units but as something that can change and be manipulated. The scientific method is often used as a model for transaction learning. John Dewey (1938/1969) noted that the scientific method is

> the only authentic means at our command for getting at the significance of our everyday experiences of the world in which we live ... Consequently, whatever the level of experience, we have no choice but either to operate in accord with the pattern it provides or else to neglect the place of intelligence in the development and control of a living and moving experience. (p. 88)

The transaction position can be characterized by an emphasis on dialogue between teacher and student (figure 1.3). However, this dialogue stresses cognitive interactions since analysis is stressed more than synthesis and thinking more than feeling. Teaching models that are based in the transaction position usually have some set of procedures for inquiry and problem solving. Sometimes these procedures are rooted in a particular discipline such as physics or history, or alternatively they are more generalized as found in various thinking skills models. The learner is generally seen as rational and capable of intelligent behaviour or as *problem solver*.

Figure 1.3 Transaction Position

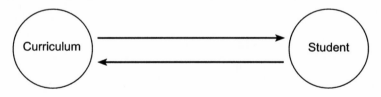

TRANSFORMATION POSITION

Transformational learning acknowledges the wholeness of the child (figure 1.4). The curriculum and child are no longer seen as separate but as connected.

The aim of the transformation position is the development of the whole person. The student is not reduced to a set of learning competencies or thinking skills but is seen as a whole being. Certainly when we

Figure 1.4 Transformation Position

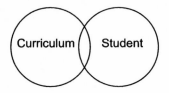

view the student as less than a whole person we diminish the opportunity for authentic learning. The teacher working from this position will use strategies such as creative problem solving, cooperative learning, and the arts, which encourage students to make various types of connections. These connections make learning personally and socially meaningful to the student.

In the transformation position we are also concerned about links with the other forms of learning. This might be diagrammed as in figure 1.5. Here the transmission position is viewed as the smallest domain while the transformation position is the most inclusive. Again, inclusiveness is another important factor in holistic learning. As long as the form of learning does not discriminate against or diminish the individual in any way, it can be included. Although this diagram is certainly not the only way the positions can be related, it represents a more holistic stance.

Figure 1.5 A Holistic Stance

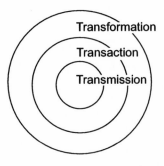

Elsewhere I have described other diagrammatic relationships of the three positions (Miller, 1993). In my classes I ask the student to diagram or picture how they see the relationship between the three positions.

I encourage the students to *play* with the three positions as a way of exploring holistic learning rather than using the system to categorize various types of learning and curricula.

Connections

Holistic education also involves exploring and making connections as it attempts to move from fragmentation to connectedness.

The focus of holistic education is on relationships: the relationship between linear thinking and intuition, the relationship between mind and body, the relationships among various domains of knowledge, the relationship between the individual and community, the relationship to the earth, and our relationship to our souls. In the holistic curriculum the student examines these relationships so that he or she gains both an awareness of them and the skills necessary to transform the relationships where it is appropriate.

This definition of holistic education centres on connection and can be explored in a number of different contexts. The connections/relationships are briefly outlined below.

LINEAR THINKING AND INTUITION

The holistic curriculum attempts to restore a balance between linear thinking and intuition. Various techniques such as metaphor and visualization can be integrated with more traditional thinking approaches so that a synthesis is achieved between analysis and intuition.

RELATIONSHIP BETWEEN MIND AND BODY

The holistic curriculum explores the relationship between mind and body so the student senses the connection between the two. This relationship can be explored through movement, dance, and drama.

RELATIONSHIPS AMONG DOMAINS OF KNOWLEDGE

There are many different ways in which we can connect academic disciplines and school subjects. For example, Waldorf education connects subjects through the arts.

RELATIONSHIP BETWEEN SELF AND COMMUNITY

The holistic curriculum sees the student in relation to community. Community refers to the classroom, the school community, the community of one's town and nation, and the global community. The student develops interpersonal skills, community service skills, and social action skills.

RELATIONSHIP TO THE EARTH

This connection can involve listening to what Thomas Berry (1988) calls the voices of the earth. Western industrialized society can no longer hear these voices, which include the sounds of animals, the rippling of the stream, or even the roar of the wind. This connection involves seeing ourselves as part of the web of life rather than separate from the earth.

RELATIONSHIP TO THE SOUL

Ultimately, the holistic curriculum lets us realize our deeper sense of self, our soul. For centuries various philosophical and spiritual traditions have discussed the two selves of human nature. One self is our ego, which is our socialized sense of who we are. It involves all the roles we play such as wife/husband, father/mother, daughter/son, as well as our job identity. Beyond this self is what has been called our soul, or what Emerson calls the 'big person.' The soul opens to us when we hear a piece of music, see a child at play, are deeply involved in our work, or are simply being present in nature. Our ego sees self as separate from everyone else and often competing with others in a never-ending struggle. There is no struggle for the soul since it senses a deep connection to others and all life. It realizes separation is an illusion exposed by a fundamental unity.

In summary, holistic education is an education of balance (for example, right relationship), inclusion, and connection.

References

Aurelius, M. (1997). *Meditations*. Mineola, NY: Dover.

Bateson, G., & Bateson, M.C. (1987). *Angels fear: Towards an epistemology of the sacred*. New York: Macmillan.

Berry, T. (1988). *The dream of the earth*. San Francisco: Sierra Club Books.

Boldt, L.G. (1999). *The tao of abundance: Eight ancient principles for abundant living*. New York: Penguin/Arkana

Campbell, J. (1986). *The inner reaches of outer space: Metaphor as myth and as religion*. New York: Alfred van der Marck.

Capra, F. (1996). *The web life: A new scientific understanding of living systems.* New York: Doubleday

Dewey, J. *Experience and education.* (1969). New York: Macmillan/Collier Books. (Original work published in 1938).

Easterbrook, G. (2003). *The progress paradox: How life gets better while people feel worse.* New York: Random House.

Emerson, R.W. (1990). *Selected essays, lectures, and poems.* New York: Bantam.

Hirsch, E.D., Jr, Kett, J.F., & Trefil, J. (1988). *The dictionary of cultural literacy.* Boston: Houghton Mifflin.

Miller, J.P. (1993). Worldviews, educational orientations and holistic education. In R. Miller (Ed.), *The renewal of meaning in education: Responses to the cultural and ecological crisis of our times* (pp. 53–67). Brandon, VT: Holistic Education Press.

Miller, J.P. & Seller, W. (1985). *Curriculum: Perspectives and practice.* New York: Longman

Quindlen, A. (2005, June 13). Testing: One, two three. *Newsweek,* 88.

Samuels, M. & Samuels, N. (1975). *Seeing with the mind's eye.* New York: Random House/The Bookworks.

Senge, P.M. (1990). *The fifth discipline: The art and practice of the learning organization.* New York: Doubleday.

Senge, P., Scharmer, C., Jaworski, J., and Flowers, B. (2005). *Presence: An exploration of profound change in people, organizations, and society.* New York: Doubleday.

Tolle, E. (2005). *A new earth: Awakening to your life's purpose.* New York: Dutton.

CHAPTER TWO

The Philosophic Context:
The Perennial Philosophy

The 'perennial philosophy' (Huxley, 1970) provides the philosophic underpinnings of the holistic curriculum. The perennial philosophy holds that all life is connected in an interdependent universe. Stated differently, we experience relatedness through a fundamental ground of being.

The Perennial Philosophy

The roots of holistic education can be found in a core wisdom underlying various spiritual traditions and teachings. This core wisdom is referred to as the *perennial philosophy*. It is possible to identify the perennial philosophy, or at least aspects of it, within the mystical thread of most religions and spiritual psychologies. In the West the search for the perennial philosophy can be traced to thinkers such as Plotinus and Augustine. In the East it has it roots in the Upanishads, the Tao te Ching, and the teachings of the Buddha. The term was first used by Agostino Steuco in referring to the work of the Renaissance philosopher Marsilio Ficino. Leibniz picked up this thread in the eighteenth century. In the last century Aldous Huxley (1970) wrote a book on this topic. His brief definition of the perennial philosophy is:

> the metaphysic that recognizes a divine Reality substantial to the world of things and lives and minds; the psychology that finds in the soul something similar to, or even identical with, divine Reality; the ethic that places man's final end in the knowledge of the immanent and transcendent Ground of all being – the thing is immemorial and universal. (p. vii)

More recently Ken Wilber (1997) has written extensively about the perennial philosophy.

It is important not to approach the perennial philosophy in a reductionistic manner (Ferrer, 2002). The universality of the perennial philosophy must also respect the diversity of spiritual traditions and practices. Ferrer calls for a 'more relaxed universalism' that acknowledges the mysterious relationship between the one and many. It is within this spirit that I attempt to outline in more detail the major principles of the perennial philosophy. Although Ferrer is critical of the term 'perennial' philosophy, I think it is possible to have a relaxed universalism, using the term 'perennial' but bringing a stronger awareness and respect for pluralistic approaches to spirituality and spiritual practices. For this purpose I draw on the following individuals: Gandhi (Hinduism), the Dalai Lama (Buddhism), Emerson (transcendentalism), and Thomas Merton (Christian mysticism).

Anna Lemkow (1990) has identified an important paradox in relation to the perennial philosophy:

> A paradoxical feature of the perennial philosophy is that it is perennial, a recurrent yet open-ended wisdom that develops commensurately with the evolution of human consciousness. For, as Lama Anagarika Govinda stated in another context, wisdom is not merely an intellectually formulated doctrine, proclaimed at a certain point in human history, but a movement which reveals its deepest nature in contact with different conditions and circumstances of human life and on every new level of human consciousness. (p. 24)

So the relaxed universalism of Ferrer and the perennial philosophy are not static but dynamic and manifest in 'different conditions and circumstances.' Lemkow's book is an important foundational text in holism that explores the meaning of wholeness in relation to science, religion, and society.

In my view the perennial philosophy contains the following elements:

1. There is an interconnectedness of reality and a mysterious unity (e.g., Huxely's divine reality) in the universe.
2. There is an intimate connection between the individual's inner self, or soul, and this mysterious unity.

3. Knowledge of this mysterious unity can be developed through various contemplative practices.
4. Values are derived from seeing and realizing the interconnectedness of reality.
5. This realization can lead to social activity designed to counter injustice and human suffering

The Interconnected Nature of Reality and the Mysterious Unity of the Universe

The perennial philosophy acknowledges diversity and the fact that the universe is in process; however, underlying diversity and change is unity. This unity is not monistic; instead, the emphasis is on the relationships between the whole and the part, or the one and the many, which I described briefly in the previous chapter. In fact, it is this relationship that is at the heart of the perennial philosophy. Ferrer refers to Martin Buber (1970) and Paul Mendes-Flohr (1989) and the realm of 'the Between,' which is the place between objects. This is the mysterious nature of relationship and of the divine unity. Also, relationship is not static but dynamic. David Bohm (1980) referred to this as holomovement, which, he says, is 'undefinable and immeasurable' (p.151).

For Gandhi (1980), this unity reveals itself in the immediacy of daily life, and he claims that this unity lies behind all religions. He said:

> The forms are many, but the informing spirit is one. How can there be room for distinctions of high and low where there is this all-embracing fundamental unity underlying the outward diversity? For that is a fact meeting you at every step in daily life. The final goal of all religions is to realize this essential oneness. (p. 63)

Gandhi's position, that this unity is evident in everyday life, reflects the notion that the interconnectedness of reality should not be relegated to remote forms of mysticism.

Interconnectedness and interdependence also lie at the heart of Buddhism. In speaking about concepts, the Dalai Lama (1995) says: 'We will find that many of our concepts indicate a very deep, very complex inter-connectedness. For instance, when we speak of ourselves as subjects, we can make sense of that notion only in relation to an object – the idea of a subject makes sense only in relation to an object' (p.110).

Einstein (1984) spoke of a cosmic religion that involves an awareness of the harmony of nature:

> The individual feels the sublimity and marvelous order which reveal themselves both in nature and in the world of thought. Individual existence impresses him as a sort of prison and he wants to experience the universe as a single significant whole. (p. 102)

The Intimate Connection between the Individual's Inner Self, or Soul, and the Mysterious Unity

In his journal Emerson (1909–14) stated:

> A man finds out that there is somewhat in him that knows more than he does. Then he comes presently to the curious question, Who's who? which of these two is really me? the one that knows more or the one that knows less: the little fellow or the big fellow. (p. 190)

Emerson's little fellow is our personal ego, which strives to impose its will on the universe. The big fellow, which is referred to as the Atman (Hinduism), Kingdom of God within (Christianity) and Buddha nature (Buddhism), realizes the futility of such endeavours and merely seeks to be in tune with the unity. When we are in touch with the 'big fellow,' we 'are not to do, but let do, not to work, but to be worked upon.' With the little fellow, we strive and manipulate; with the big fellow, we listen and see and, according to Emerson, are subject to a 'vast and sudden enlargement of power' (p. 190). Emerson is referring to the creative power that is similar to Einstein's cosmic religion that inspires the artist and the scientist.

Gandhi (1980) described the relationship between the individual soul and the cosmos in this way:

> I believe in the absolute oneness of God and, therefore, of humanity. What though we have many bodies? We have but one soul. The rays of the sun are many through refraction. But they have the same source. I cannot, therefore, detach myself from the wickedest soul nor may I be denied identity with the most virtuous. (p. 72)

For Gandhi the connection with God leads to the connection with all humanity.

Wisdom or Knowledge of the Mysterious Unity Can Be Developed through Various Contemplative Practices

A consistent thread in the perennial philosophy is that the rational mind, which focuses on analysis, cannot fully grasp the wholeness of existence. Instead, intuition should be cultivated in order to see more clearly the interrelatedness of reality. Gandhi (1980) refers to intuition as that 'still small voice within' that prods him to social action: 'There are moments in your life when you must act, even though you cannot carry your best friends with you. The "still small voice" within you must always be the final arbiter when there is conflict of duty' (p. 62).

Specific approaches have been advocated to cultivate intuition. These methods, which include contemplative practices (e.g., meditation), body work, and loving service, have been developed to help one to 'see.' Again, this seeing is usually a gradual awakening to the interconnectedness of things.

Emerson, for example, suggested that it was helpful to be quiet and to listen. In this quiet, we can gain access to the 'infinitude' within each person. Gandhi (1980) believed that silence was helpful in seeking God. He said:

> It [silence] has now become both a physical and spiritual necessity for me. Originally it was taken to relieve the sense of pressure. Then I wanted time for writing. After, however, I had practiced it for some time, I saw the spiritual value of it. It suddenly flashed across my mind that that was the time when I could best hold communion with God. And now I feel as though I was naturally built for silence. (p. 101)

The contemplation of Emerson, however, is different from Gandhi's meditation. In Eastern practices meditation tends to be more focused (e.g., repeating a mantra or counting one's breath) than contemplation, which is more unstructured. It is important to realize the diversity of methods used to come in contact with the unity and not assign priority to any one method or practice (Ferrer, 2002).

Values Are Derived from Seeing and Realizing the Interconnectedness of Reality

Values are derived from realizing the fundamental connectedness between individuals; in other words, values are linked to relatedness.

Positive values enhance or realize relatedness, and negative values foster separateness and paranoia. Compassion, for example, is a central value in the perennial philosophy. The Dalai Lama consistently refers to the importance of compassion. If we experience interconnectedness and interdependence, a natural sense of compassion for all beings tends to arise. Not seeing ourselves as separate, we feel a basic connection to living beings, both human and non-human. According to the Dalai Lama,

> compassion is based on a clear acceptance or recognition that others, like oneself, want happiness and have the right to overcome suffering. On that basis one develops some kind of concern about the welfare of others, irrespective of one's attitude to oneself. That is compassion. (p. 63)

He also refers to the importance of compassion and loving kindness in all relationships including teaching. At one point he says: 'it is my experience that those lessons which we learn from teachers who are not just good, but who also show affection for the student, go deep into our minds' (p. 60). He adds: 'compassion for the students' lives or futures not only for their examinations, makes your work as a teacher much more effective' (p. 72).

Thomas Merton (1959) also wrote about compassion which arises out of a sensitivity to another's inner life. He said: 'Compassion and respect enable us to know the solitude of another by finding him in the intimacy of our own interior solitude' (p. 135).

An Awareness of the Mysterious Unity of Existence Leads to Social Action to Counter Injustice and Human Suffering

This last principle is usually not included in descriptions of the perennial philosophy, but I believe it arises from the other principles. If human beings realize they are part of a fundamental unity, then they naturally feel a connectedness and responsibility to others. Most important is the idea that social reform should start from within. According to Emerson (1903–4),

> the origin of all reform is in that mysterious fountain of the moral sentiment in man, which, amidst the natural, ever contains the supernatural for men. That is new and creative. That is alive. That alone can make a man other than he is. (Vol. 3, p. 272)

Emerson's 'moral sentiment' is analogous to his 'big fellow,' which is connected to something bigger than oneself. Although Emerson was not a social activist, he spoke out against slavery and particularly against Daniel Webster's support of the Fugitive Slave Law. He also opposed the exclusion of the Cherokee Indians from Georgia and supported women's rights.

Gandhi, of course, was a social activist who used *ahimsa* (non-violence) and *satyagraha* (soul force) as vehicles for social change. For Gandhi (1980), religion and politics cannot be compartmentalized:

> I could not be leading a religious life unless I identified myself with the whole of mankind, and that I could not do unless I took part in politics. The whole gamut of man's activities today constitutes an indivisible whole. You cannot divide social, economic, political and purely religious work into watertight compartments. I do not know any religion apart from human activity. It provides a moral basis to all other activities which they would otherwise lack, reducing life to a maze of 'sound and fury signifying nothing.' (p. 63)

Based on his holistic perspective, Gandhi did act to relieve the suffering of his people and to help India become independent of British rule. What is instructive about Gandhi is that his social activity tended to be self-based rather than ego-based. The famous salt march to the sea is a good example of this, as the idea for the march came to him in a dream one night after months of meditation and reflection. Some people (Fischer, 1954) have argued that the salt march was the most important event leading to Indian independence.

Merton (1959) wrote about a 'theology of love' which must address injustice in the world. He said this theology 'must seek to deal realistically with the evil and injustice in the world, and not merely to compromise with them ... Theology does not exist merely to appease the already too untroubled conscience of the powerful and the established' (p. 129).

If the perennial philosophy focuses solely on spiritual practices without reference to the relief of suffering then there is the danger of narcissism. Ultimately, the perennial philosophy and related practices should lead to an active and dynamic love. This love arises from a deep sense of connection to the earth, all living beings, and the cosmos.

Conclusion

It is fitting to close this chapter with Gandhi's (1980) conception of education, since I relied on his work in outlining the perennial philosophy. It is, I believe, one of the best definitions of holistic education:

> I hold that true education of the intellect can only come through a proper exercise and training of the bodily organs, e.g., hands, feet, eyes, ears, nose, etc. In other words an intelligent use of the bodily organs in a child provides the best and quickest way of developing his intellect. But unless the development of the mind and body goes hand in hand with a corresponding awakening of the soul, the former alone would prove to be a poor lopsided affair. By spiritual training I mean education of the heart. A proper and all round development of the mind, therefore, can take place only when it proceeds *pari passu* with the education of the physical and spiritual faculties of the child. They constitute an indivisible whole. According to this theory, therefore, it would be a gross fallacy to suppose that they can be developed piecemeal or independently of one another. (p. 138)

Here is a vision of education that is radically different from the one we see proposed by governments and the media today. Based as it is in the core wisdom of the perennial philosophy, I find it deeply inspiring.

References

Buber, M. (1970). *I and thou*. (W. Kaufman, Trans.). New York: Scribner.

Bohm, D. (1980). *Wholeness and the implicate order*. London: Routledge & Kegan Paul.

Dalai Lama (1995). *The power of compassion*. San Francisco: Thorsons.

Einstein, A. (1984). Cosmic religious feeling. In K. Wilber (Ed.), *Quantum questions: Mystical writings of the world's great physicists* (pp. 101–5). Boulder, CO: Shambhala. (Reprinted from *Ideas and Opinions*, by A. Einstein, 1954, New York: Crown).

Emerson, R.W. (1903–4). *The complete works*. Vol. 3. Boston: Houghton Mifflin.

Emerson, R.W. (1909–14). *The journals of Ralph Waldo Emerson*. Vol. 9. Boston: Houghton Mifflin.

Ferrer, J.N. (2002). *Revisioning transpersonal theory: A participatory vision of human spirituality.* Albany, NY: SUNY Press.

Fischer, L. (1954). *Gandhi: His life and message for the world.* New York: Mentor.

Gandhi, M. (1980). *All men are brothers: Autobiographical reflections.* K. Kripalani (Ed.). New York: Continuum.

Huxley, A. (1970). *The perennial philosophy.* New York: Harper Colophon.

Lemkow, A. (1990). *The wholeness principle: Dynamics of unity with science, religion, and society.* Wheaton, IL: Theosophical Publishing House.

Mendes-Flohr, P. (1989). *From mysticism to dialogue: Martin Buber's transformation of German social thought.* Detroit: Wayne State University Press.

Merton, T. (1959). *The inner experience.* Unpublished manuscript, fourth draft.

Wilber, K. (1997). *The eye of the spirit: An integral vision for a world gone slightly mad.* Boston: Shambhala.

CHAPTER THREE

The Psychological Context:
The Unconditioned Self

The perennial philosophy is based on the concept that within each human being is a conditioned self, or soul. This is the deepest part of being, which at the same time is connected to the highest principle of the universe – God, or the Tao. Hinduism refers to the Atman (individual consciousness)–Brahman (universal consciousness) connection. Before examining the soul in more detail, let us briefly review the three educational orientations discussed in chapter 1 and their psychologies and focus. This is done in the form of a chart:

Position	Psychology	Location	Focus
Transmission	Behavioural	Body	Behaviour
Transaction	Cognitive	Mind	Intelligence
Transformation	Transpersonal	Soul	Wisdom

Behavioural psychology ignores the inner life of the person and is concerned only with environment and behaviour. Stimuli and reinforcements influence how a person acts; for example, positive reinforcement is used to increase the frequency of a particular behaviour while negative reinforcement is designed to decrease the frequency of a behaviour.

Cognitive psychology focuses on cognition and intelligence. In most cases, it centres on what Gardner (1983) calls logical-mathematical intelligence. Logical-mathematical intelligence is what Piaget studied in his own work. No mention is made of spiritual intelligence, or wisdom, which is one of the main goals of transpersonal psychology. Wisdom is intelligence rooted in the soul. The ancients call this the 'thinking heart.' Wisdom links intuition and intelligence in order to deal with the large questions: What is our role in the universe? How can we deal with human suffering?

Transpersonal psychology has two sources. One source is the mystical traditions within the major faiths of Christianity, Buddhism, Islam, Hinduism, and Judaism. The other source includes psychologies such as Jungian psychology and psychosynthesis, which have a spiritual element. We will now turn to the conceptions of the soul within the major spiritual traditions.

Conceptions of the Soul

Christianity

Jesus continually referred to the kingdom of God; but what are the characteristics of this kingdom? First of all, it is within us (Luke 17.21). Jesus used parables to elaborate on the meaning of this kingdom. He said:

> The kingdom of heaven is like treasure hidden in a field which someone has found; he hides it again, goes off happy, sells everything he owns and buys the field. (Matthew 13.44)

The kingdom, then, is something that is discovered within. In order to discover it one needs a certain way of seeing. One needs to drop all conditioning and become like a child (Mark 9.35-7). Jesus was critical of the Pharisees, who followed elaborate rules and laws; instead, he advocated a radical awakening. He said:

> For I tell you, if your virtue goes no deeper than that of the Scribes and Pharisees, you will never get into the kingdom of heaven. (Matthew 5.20)

Here, Jesus is clearly referring to profound inner transformation. Once this transformation has begun, he compares the growth of soul (the kingdom of God) to other images of growth:

> The kingdom of heaven is like a mustard seed which a man took and sowed in his field. It is the smallest of all the seeds, but when it has grown it is the biggest shrub of all and becomes a tree so that the birds of the air come and shelter in its branches. (Matthew 13.31-2; Mark 4.30-2; Luke 13.18-19)

The kingdom of heaven is like the yeast a woman took and mixed in with three measures of flour till it was leavened all through. (Matthew 13.33; Luke 13.20–1)

When realized within us, the kingdom of God leads to wholeness. Jesus often said 'Your faith has made you whole.'

Different mystics and sages have elaborated on Jesus's conception of the kingdom within us. Augustine, Eckhart, Teresa, John Wesley, and Thomas Merton are among the few who have referred to our spiritual centre. They have called it the soul, the eye of the soul, the ground of being, the heart, the transcendental self (McNamara, 1975). Generally, Christians hold that our soul is not God but the point within us where God touches us. In other words, it is where we and God meet.

Merton (1959) develops the concept of the unconditioned self in an unpublished manuscript called *The Inner Experience*. Merton calls this the 'inner self' and contrasts it to our ego, or the exterior 'I.' He says:

But the exterior 'I,' the 'I' of projects, of temporal finalities, the 'I' that manipulates objects in order to take possession of them, is alien from the hidden, interior 'I' who has no projects and seeks to accomplish nothing, even contemplation. He seeks only to be, and to move (for he is dynamic) according to the secret laws of Being itself, and according to the promptings of a Superior Freedom (that is, of God), rather than to plan and to achieve according to his own desires. (pp. 4–5)

In contrast, the inner self of 'I' is characterized by the capacity for the deepest connection with others:

The inner 'I' is certainly the sanctuary of our most personal and individual solitude, and yet, paradoxically, it is precisely that which is most solitary and personal in ourselves which is united with the 'Thou' who confronts us. We are not capable of union with one another on the deepest level until the inner self in each one of us is sufficiently awakened to confront the inmost spirit of the other. (p. 20)

How can we awaken the inner self? Merton suggests that we can awaken the inner self through contemplation and love. He also argues that the two are closely related:

In fact, contemplation is man's highest and most essential spiritual activity. It is his most creative and dynamic affirmation of his divine sonship ... Solitude is necessary for spiritual freedom. But once that freedom is acquired, it demands to be put to work in the service of a love in which there is no longer subjection or slavery. Mere withdrawal, without the return to freedom in action, would lead to a static and death-like inertia of the spirit in which the inner self would not awaken at all. (p. 22)

Merton, then, refers to a balance between contemplation and service to others. If we become too inward-oriented, we lose touch with others; however, if we become too caught up in the external world, then we can become lost in the exterior 'I' and the delusions of our ego.

Judaism

The unconditioned self is also found within Judaism. When Moses saw the burning bush on Mt Horeb, he encountered his soul:

And Moses said unto God: 'Behold when I come unto the children of Israel, and shall say unto them: The God of your fathers hath sent me unto you; and they shall say to me: What is His name? What shall I say unto them?' And God said unto Moses: ' I AM THAT I AM'; and He said: 'Thus shalt thou say unto the children of Israel: I AM hath sent me unto you.' (Exodus 3.13–14)

The 'I AM' is another name for our soul.

There is also an ancient mystical strand within Judaism known as the Kabbalah (Hoffman, 1980), which acknowledges that there is a part within us that is connected to the divine. The Kabbalah states that there are three aspects to each person: (1) *nefesh*, a type of biological energy; (2) the *ruah*, or spirit, which is another name for the individual's psyche; and (3) *neshamah*, or the self, which unites the person with the universal divine essence. The Kabbalah recommends techniques similar to various eastern spiritual practices in the attempt to reach this unity. For example, according to Scholem (1961), Abraham Abulafia, the Kabbalist of the thirteenth century, advocated yogic postures, breathing exercises, and meditation. Other Kabbalistic practices have involved the recitation of special rhythmic prayers that are similar to Hindu mantras. For example, it is recommended that the person meditate on the inner sound of 'Aleph,' the first letter of the Hebrew alphabet.

Buddhism

Buddhism posits that our selves or egos are an illusion; instead, Buddhists refer to our true nature as our Buddha-nature. Bodhidarma, the Indian Buddhist sage who brought Buddhism to China in the sixth century A.D., said: 'If you wish to seek the Buddha, you ought to see into your own Nature for this Nature is the Buddha himself' (as cited in Suzuki, 1956, p. 87). As in the other spiritual traditions, the person needs to look inwards. Bodhidarma said: 'If, instead of seeing into your own Nature, you turn away to seek the Buddha in external things, you will never get at him' (p. 88).

Chih, a Chinese Buddhist monk of the eighth century A.D., described one's true self in this way: 'This Nature is from the first pure and undefiled, serene and undisturbed. It belongs to no categories of duality such as being and non-being, pure and defiled, long and short, taking in and giving up; the Body remains in its suchness. To have a clear insight into this is to see one's Self-nature. Therefore, seeing into one's Self-nature is becoming the Buddha' (as cited in Suzuki, 1956, p. 206).

Generally, Buddhists see the unconditioned self as empty and interconnected with all things and all life. Many Buddhists don't even like to use the word self or soul. It is important to realize that when one uses the term self or soul, it is simply as a metaphor for relinquishing our sense of separateness and acknowledging that we exist without boundaries.

Chogyam Trungpa (1984) described Buddha-nature as a basic goodness. He says, 'Every human being has a basic nature of goodness, which is undiluted and unconfused. That goodness contains tremendous gentleness and appreciation' (p. 30). Trungpa goes on to describe how this goodness can unfold:

> The basic point is that, when you live your life in accordance with basic goodness, then you develop natural elegance. Your life can be spacious and relaxed, without having to be sloppy. You can actually let go of your depression and embarrassment about being a human being, and you can cheer up. You don't have to blame the world for your problems. You can relax and appreciate the world. (p. 32)

How can we access this basic goodness? Again meditation is the main vehicle:

> Our life is an endless journey; it is like a broad highway that extends infinite-

ly into the distance. The practice of meditation provides a vehicle to travel on that road. Our journey consists of constant ups and downs, hope and fear, but it is a good journey. The practice of meditation allows us to experience all the textures of the roadway, which is what the journey is all about. Through the practice of meditation, we begin to find that within ourselves there is no fundamental complaint about anything or anyone at all. (p. 84)

Hinduism

As mentioned earlier, Hinduism views the connection between individual and universal consciousness as Atman-Brahman. The purpose of spiritual practice is to discover the Atman within oneself. When this is done, union with Brahman is also realized. Krishna in the *Bhagavad Gita* describes the Atman in the following manner:

Know this Atman
Unborn, undying,
Never ceasing,
Never beginning,
Deathless, birthless,
Unchanging for ever.
How can It die
The death of the body?

Knowing It birthless,
Knowing It deathless,
Knowing It endless,
For ever unchanging,
Dream not you do
The deed of the killer,
Dream not the power
Is yours to command it.

Worn-out garments
Are shed by the body:
Worn-out bodies
Are shed by the dweller
Within the body.
New bodies are donned
By the dweller, like garments.

Not wounded by weapons,
Not burned by fire,
Not dried by the wind,
Not wetted by water:
Such is the Atman,

Not dried, not wetted,
Not burned, not wounded,
Innermost element,
Everywhere, always,
Being of beings,
Changeless, eternal,
For ever and ever. (Cited in Johnson, 1971, pp. 56–7)

How does one realize the Atman? The mystic literature of Hinduism, or the *Vedanta*, describes four methods by which a person can attain union (yoga) with God.

One form is *karma yoga*. Karma yoga is the path of selfless service where we offer the fruits of our work to God. In one's daily life the person offers his or her work to God and thus becomes pure in heart.

Jnana yoga is the way to God realization through the intellect. The person learns to discriminate between the eternal and the non-eternal. By learning to discriminate between the eternal and non-eternal, the individual focuses his life on the eternal and thus realizes the Atman within.

The path of devotion is *bakhti yoga*. People who follow this path fill their hearts with love for the divine. For example, the devotee may repeat the name of God in order to merge with the divine.

Raja yoga is a fourth path where the individual focuses on meditation as vehicle for union. Here the yogi develops one-pointedness of mind so that he or she can concentrate fully on God.

It is possible that a yogi may use all these methods, but probably he or she will concentrate on one method as the main vehicle for union. The choice will depend to some extent on the temperament of the yogi.

Islam

To examine the unconditioned self in Islam, I would like to turn to Sufism, which is a mystic form of the Islamic faith. Sufism was a reaction to overintellectualism and legalism in some forms of Islam. Sufism claims that God can be experienced by light, knowledge, and love. Divine union, or 'Tawhid,' has two main stages: (1) 'Fana,' or the extinction of the ego; and (2) 'Ba'qa,' or reintegration in God. Al-Ghazali, the Islamic theologian of the twelfth century made Sufism more acceptable within orthodox Islam. Jalaudin Rumi, the thirteenth-century Sufi, was a famous poet who also founded the Melvlevi order of 'whirling dervishes.' The dervish uses the dance as well as repeating the Name of God, Allah, to realize self. Rumi said this about the search for God:

> Cross and Christians, end to end, I examined. He was not on the Cross.
> I went to the Hindu temple, to the ancient pagoda. In none of them was
> there any sign. To the uplands of Herat I went, and to Kandahar. I looked.
> He was not on the heights or in the lowlands. Resolutely, I went to the
> summit of the (fabulous) mountain of Kaf. There only was the dwelling
> of the (legendary) Anqu bird. I went to the Kaaba of Mecca. He was not
> there. I asked about him from Avicenna, the philosopher. He was beyond
> the range of Avicenna ... I looked into my own heart. In that place, I saw
> him. He was in no other place. (Shah, 1970, p. 105)

One of the main ways to Wisdom for the Sufi is storytelling. The following story is a metaphorical description of the unconditioned self:

The Tale of the Sands

A stream, from its source in far-off mountains, passing through every kind and description of countryside, at last reached the sands of the desert. Just as it had crossed every other barrier, the stream tried to cross this one, but it found that as fast as it ran into the sand, its waters disappeared.

It was convinced, however, that its destiny was to cross this desert, and that there was no way. Now a hidden voice, coming from the desert itself, whispered: 'The wind crosses the desert, and so can the stream.'

The stream objected that it was dashing itself against the sand, and only getting absorbed: that the wind could fly and this was why it could cross a desert.

'By hurtling in your own accustomed way you cannot get across. You will either disappear or become a marsh. You must allow the wind to carry you over, to your destination.'

But how could this happen? 'By allowing yourself to be absorbed in the wind.'

This idea was not acceptable to the stream. After all, it had never been absorbed before. It did not want to lose its individuality. And, once having lost it, how was one to know that it could ever be regained?

'The wind,' said the sand, 'performs this function. It takes up water, carries it over the desert, and then lets it fall again. Falling as rain, the water again becomes a river.'

'How can I know that this is true?'

'It is so, and if you do not believe it, you cannot become more than a quagmire, and even that could take many, many years; and it certainly is not the same as a stream.'

'But can I not remain the same stream that I am today?'

'You cannot in either case remain so,' the whisper said. 'Your essential part is carried away and forms a stream again. You are called what you are even today because you do not know which part of you is the essential one.'

When he heard this, certain echoes began to arise in the thoughts of the stream. Dimly, he remembered a state in which he or some part of him, was it? had been held in the arms of a wind. He also remembered or did he? that this was the real thing, not necessarily the obvious thing to do.

And the stream raised his vapour into the welcoming arms of the wind, which gently and easily bore it upwards and along, letting it fall softly as soon as they reached the roof of a mountain, many, many miles away. And because he had had his doubts, the stream was able to remember and record more strongly in his mind the details of the experience. He reflected, 'Yes, now I have learned my true identity.'

The stream was learning. But the sands whispered: 'We know, because we see it happen day after day: and because we, the sands, extend from the riverside all the way to the mountain.'

And that is why it is said that the way in which the Stream of Life is to continue on its journey is written in the Sands. (Shah, 1971, pp. 23–4)

Indigenous Religions

Indigenous people believe that all things are invested with spirit. Thus religion, or more appropriately spirituality, infuses all aspects of life. There is no separation of life into compartments; everything is seen as related and connected. Knudston and Suzuki (1992) in their book on Native wisdom make this point:

> The Native Mind tends to view the universe as the dynamic interplay of elusive and ever-changing natural forces, not as a vast array of static physical objects.
>
> The landscape itself, or certain regions of it, is seen as sacred and quivering with life. (p. 13)

Because indigenous people see spirit in everything, they are imbued with a deep sense of reverence for nature. They see themselves in mutual relationship with earth and its habitants and feel a responsibility to help preserve and care for both:

> The Native Mind tends to emphasize celebration of and participation in the orderly designs of nature instead of rationally 'dissecting the world.'
>
> It tends to reveal a profound sense of empathy and kinship with other forms of life rather than a sense of separateness from them or superiority over them. (p. 15)

The Inuit of northern Canada believe that each being, including animals, has a soul. 'They envision the soul as a tiny being, a minute version of the creature that it animates and transforms' (p. 41). As in other religions, the soul is viewed as indestructible and thus survives death.

As we face the large environmental challenges such as global warming and pollution of the oceans, the indigenous worldview is now seen as one way to help heal the planet.

Religions and the Soul

This review of how the major faiths articulate their conception of the soul is not an attempt to gloss over differences in conceptions. Even within the various faiths there are disputes about the nature of the person and his or her relationship to God. For example, in Christianity the monastic and contemplative traditions have not been predominant. Yet there does seem to be more similarities than differences among the mystical strains of the faiths. Again, these commonalities have formed the core of the perennial philosophy.

Psychology and the Self

We turn now to various psychologies and their descriptions of the self.

Jung

Jung's conception of the self is diagrammed in figure 3.1. The ego is seen as a small illuminated area in the larger, dark sphere of the psyche. The ego is the individual's conscious awareness that views the images that come from both within the psyche and without. The self or soul lies at the centre of the psyche and is the 'inventor, organizer, and source of dream images' (Jung, 1968, p. 161). Jung suggests that the self can send images to the ego and that these images are important to the person's spiritual development. Thus, the person needs to turn inward to hear the messages of the soul. Jung (1933) suggests that an image can surface when an individual is confronting a problem or provide inspiration for artistic activity.

Figure 3.1 Jung's Conception of the Self

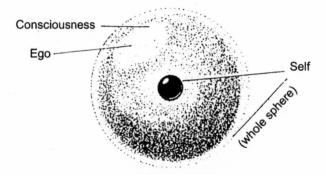

The soul is also closely linked with what Jung called the 'collective unconscious.' The collective unconscious is the source of universal archetypes and images that often can arise within the soul and reveal issues and themes in our lives. Again, there is no boundary between self and the collective unconscious. As in the Atman–Brahman connection, one is simply a microcosm of the whole.

Psychosynthesis

Robert Assagioli, the founder of psychosynthesis, articulated the concept of the higher or transpersonal self. Figure 3.2 is a diagram of Assagioli's conception of consciousness.

Figure 3.2 Assagioli's Concept of Consciousness

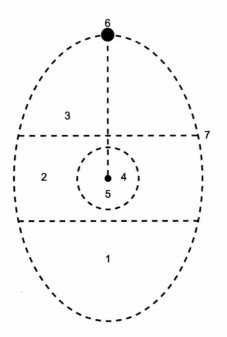

1. Lower unconsciousness
2. Middle unconsciousness
3. Superconsciousness
4. Field of consciousness
5. Personal self, or 'I'
6. Transpersonal self
7. Collective unconsciousness

The lower unconscious represents the person's psychological past in terms of repressions and distant memories. Psychosynthesis attempts to tap these memories. If they are ignored, the repressed energy can lead to neurosis and dysfunction.

The middle unconscious (2) is our present state of mind and is applied to our field of consciousness (4). Our field of consciousness is what we perceive at the present moment.

Our potential future is represented by the superconscious (3). Here we receive our highest intuitions and inspirations: 'artistic, philosophical or scientific, ethical imperatives and urges to humanitarian and heroic action. It is the source of higher feelings, such as altruistic love; of genius and the states of contemplation, illumination and ecstasy' (Assagioli, 1965, pp. 17–18).

These three levels of consciousness can be viewed in a developmental or evolutionary sense in which the lower unconscious is seen as an early stage of development and the superconscious as a more evolved form of awareness. Assagioli was influenced by Jung and saw the individual psyche surrounded by the collective unconscious (7). All individuals, then, are connected through this collectivity.

Assagioli makes the distinction between our personal self and our transpersonal self. The former is our ego, which is defined by our personal desires and our social role. The transpersonal self, however, is not bound by personal ambition but has a holistic vision that connects the psyche with the universal.

Psychosynthesis has developed a number of techniques to work with different parts of the psyche. Piero Ferrucci (1982) describes a number of these techniques in *What We May Be*. One of the techniques is visualization; below is one example:

The Diamond

Vividly imagine a diamond.
See all its shining facets, perfectly integrated into one whole.
See the perfection of its shape.
  Hold the diamond in front of your inner eye, and let yourself be pervaded by its crystalline beauty.
  The word 'diamond' comes from the Greek *adamas*, 'unconquerable.' As you identify with this diamond, sense it connecting you to that part of you which is likewise unconquerable, your Self.
  Your Self is unconquerable by fear, by obscurity, by the pulls and the pushes of everyday conditioning. It is untouched by the shadows of the past, the monsters of worry, the phantoms of the future, the demons of greed, the dictatorship of social conformity. It is your very essence, shining through innumerable facets and yet one. Realize that you are that Self, and, as the image of the diamond fades away, let this sense of Self strengthen and grow ever clearer in you. (pp. 123–4)

Other exercises include identifying one's subpersonalities and dialoguing with these personalities; disidentifying with subpersonalities; dialoguing with one's inner guide, or self; working with one's will; focusing attention; and contemplating ideal qualities (e.g., Joy, Gratitude, Love, etc.). Some of these techniques will be described more fully in the second part of this book.

Ken Wilber

Ken Wilber has become one of the principal figures in transpersonal psychology. His voluminous output has presented various models of human and spiritual development. In his early work he developed what he called a spectrum of consciousness. Later he focused more on hierarchical growth, in which one develops through stages and the self is realized through this progression. Wilber presented a developmental model of consciousness. Figure 3.3 compares Wilber's model of development with the models developed by Maslow, Kohlberg, and Piaget. Below are brief descriptions of Wilber's developmental levels.

Figure 3.3   Comparison of Wilber's, Maslow's, Kohlberg's, and Piaget's Developmental Models

Wilber	Maslow	Kohlberg	Piaget
Causal			
Subtle	Self-transcendence		
Psychic	Self-actualization	Self-chosen ethical principles	
Rational	Self-esteem	Social-contract position	Formal operations
Mythic	Belongingness	Conventional morality stages 3–4	Concrete operations
Magical	Safety needs	Egocentric orientation	Pre-operations
Archaic	Physiological needs	Punishment orientation	Sensori-motor

ARCHAIC LEVEL

At the base of development is what Wilber calls the 'archaic level.' The focus of this stage is on physical sensation and emotional, sexual energy. According to Wilber, people operating at this level are dominated by their physical needs. The archaic level is parallel to Maslow's physiological-need level and Kohlberg's stage-one morality level that is organized around punishment and obedience.

MAGICAL LEVEL

At this stage of development, the person begins to think, instead of just reacting to physical needs. This stage parallels Piaget's preoperational stage, Maslow's safety-needs stage, and Kohlberg's stage-two morality level that is based on egocentric needs.

MYTHIC LEVEL

At this level, the person begins what Piaget calls concrete operational thinking; that is, he or she can figure things out without being deceived by appearances. However, the child at this level cannot reason abstractly (hypothetico-deductive reasoning). This stage corresponds to Maslow's belongingness-needs stage and Kohlberg's conventional morality stage (stages 3 and 4). In general, the person at this level is oriented toward conformity in his or her personal relations.

RATIONAL LEVEL

At this level, the person is capable of abstract thinking and also can hypothesize and rationally examine the variables which may or may not support the hypothesis. Thus, the person at the rational stage has entered Piaget's stage of formal operations. This stage correlates with Kohlberg's post-conventional morality stage and Maslow's self-esteem needs stage.

Many hierarchies of development end at this point. However, transpersonal psychologists suggest that the individual is capable of higher levels of consciousness. Wilber (1983) believes that it is reasonable to speculate in this way about the evolution of human consciousness:

> The point is that the general concept of evolution continuing beyond its present stage into some legitimately trans-rational structures is not a totally outrageous notion. Look at the course of evolution to date: from amoebas to humans! Now what if that ratio, amoeba-to-human, were applied to future evolution? That is, amoebas are to humans as humans are to What? Is it ridiculous to suggest that the 'what' might indeed be omega, geist, supermind, spirit? (p. 24)

Based on his study of mystical psychologies, Wilber has developed three stages beyond the rational.

PSYCHIC LEVEL

This is the first stage beyond the rational level. The psychic level goes beyond the rational level by forming networks of conceptual relationships. At this level, the person moves toward a higher-order synthesizing ability and makes 'connections, relates truths, coordinates ideas, integrating concepts' (Wilber, 1983, p. 27). This stage culminates in what

Aurobindo calls the 'higher mind' (p. 27). This level 'can freely express itself in single ideas, but its most characteristic movement is a mass ideation, a system of totality of truth-seeing at a single view; the relations of idea with idea, of truth with truth, self-seen in the integral whole' (p. 27). This stage is parallel to Maslow's self-actualization stage. Wilber (1983) suggests that persons at this stage can also experience insight and even illumination: 'a type of vision, noetic, numinous, inspiring, often enstatic, occasionally ecstatic' (p. 29).

SUBTLE LEVEL

At this level, the person experiences what Maslow calls self-transcendence. According to Wilber (1983), the disciplines and insights of the great saints reflect this level of development. At this level, the person experiences the highest level of intuition, that which is not emotionalism or some form of hunch, but direct spiritual insight.

CAUSAL LEVEL

This is the highest level of transpersonal development. Wilber (1983) states: 'Passing full through the state of cessation or unmanifest absorption, consciousness is said finally to re-awaken to its absolutely prior and eternal abode as spirit, radiant and all-pervading, one and many, only and all' (pp. 30-1). Here the person becomes identified with Tillich's 'Ground of Being' or Spinoza's 'Eternal Substance.' At this level, one does not have a particular set of experiences, but transcends his or her identity as the 'experiencer.' Thus, subject–object duality is transcended. Wilber labels individuals at this level as sages, drawing a distinction between saints and sages:

> As an example of the distinction between subtle saints and causal sages, we may take the Mosaic and Christic epiphanies. The Mosaic revelation on Mt. Sinai has all the standard features of a subtle level apprehension: a numinous Other that is Light, Fire, Insight, and Sound (shabd). Nowhere, however, does Moses claim to be one with or identical with that Being ... Christ, on the other hand, does claim that 'I and the Father are one,' a perfect Atmic or causal level apprehension. (pp. 31-2)

This developmental approach suggests that educators would need to match educational strategies in relation to the stage of development.

David Marshak (1997) in his book *The Common Vision* suggests that Rudolf Steiner, Sri Aurobindo, and Inayat Khan have also presented a common vision of human development. They also suggest detailed educational approaches to nourish and facilitate development. Marshak writes:

> This common vision of human becoming offers us a way to collaborate consciously with the energies of evolution – as parents and as teachers. It provides us with a template for a profoundly postmodern way to raise and educate children. (p. 2)

In one of his works, Wilber (1983) discusses a framework that is compatible with the one presented in this book. He suggests that there are three levels of knowing which correspond to the three positions outlined in this book. Wilber claims that three basic ways of knowing include sensorimotor cognition (body), mental-conceptual thought (mind), and intuition (spirit). These categories parallel the chart given at the beginning of the chapter. The first mode of knowing, which Wilber calls the eye of the flesh, can be linked with the transmission position and atomism.

The mind is the eye of reason, which participates in a world of ideas, logic, and concepts. This mode of knowing can be linked with the transaction position and pragmatism.

Finally, the spirit is the source of intuition and contemplation. Again, spirit resides in the self and can be accessed by various forms of meditation. Spirit-intuition can be linked with the transformation position and holism.

More recently Wilber has developed what he calls an integral approach, which describes four aspects to the human being: the interior and the exterior, which can then be subdivided into the individual and the collective. Figure 3.4 shows these relations as well as the theorists associated with each aspect.

Wilber (1997) elaborates on the four quadrants:

> The point is that every human being has a subjective aspect (sincerity, truthfulness), and objective aspect (truth, correspondence), an intersubjective aspect (culturally constructed meaning, justness, appropriateness), and interobjective aspect (systems and functional fit) ... The integral

Figure 3.4 Wilber's Integral Approach

	INTERIOR	EXTERIOR
	• Interpretive	• Monological
	• Hermeneutic	• Empirical, positivistic
	• Consciousness	• Form
INDIVIDUAL	Sigmund Freud C.G. Jung Jean Piaget Aurobindo Plotinus Gautama Buddha	B.F. Skinner John Watson John Locke Empiricism Behaviourism Physics, biology, neurology, etc.
	intentional	behavioural
	cultural	social
COLLECTIVE	Thomas Kuhn Wilhelm Dilthey Jean Gebser Max Weber Hans-Georg Gadamer	Systems theory Talcott Parsons Auguste Comte Karl Marx Gerhard Lenski

vision attempts instead to include the moment of truth in each of these approaches – from empiricism to constructivism to relativism to aestheticism – but, in stripping them of their claims to be the only type of truth existence, releases them from their contradictions – and places them, as it were, into a genuine rainbow coalition. (p. 29)

Tobin Hart (2002) has explored Wilber's four quadrants in relation to education. Wilber suggests that each quadrant represents a different form of truth and that the four quadrants provide a needed multi-dimensional approach. Hart suggests how looking at the solar system from the four quadrants could broaden the learning experience:

Asking about the empirical facts of the moon phase looks to the exterior-individual quadrant of knowledge and truth; considering various systems (e.g., solar, earth-moon) in interaction, including causal mechanisms (e.g., gravitational influence), touches on the exterior-systemic; inquiring about the student's subjective experience of sitting under the moon and perhaps asking for poetry, asking open-ended questions, or fantasizing touches the individual-interior; and digging into our shared attitudes about the moon, for example, by comparing cross-cultural stories about the moon and its mythology, we peek into the interior-cultural. Each has validity, each is true in its own domain, and each serves the development of knowledge. The development of structures such as the liberal arts curriculum is an attempt to respect different domains. (p. 9)

Sean Esbjorn-Hargens (in press) has written about how Wilber's ideas have inspired faculty at John F. Kennedy University to develop a graduate program that includes many of the principles of integral education.

Critiques of Wilber's work are numerous. Ferrer (2002) makes the point that Wilber endorses a reductionist methodology when he suggests that art, science, and religion 'can be brought together under one roof using the core methodology of deep empricism'(p. 56). Despite Wilber's efforts to build an integral vision, Ferrer argues instead that he has confined 'spiritual inquiry within an epistemic straightjacket' (p. 57).

Wilber has made a few comments about education, some of which I find rather disturbing. In his book *One Taste*, Wilber (1999) endorses the standards movement and attacks progressive education, which he suggests is based on 'idiot compassion' (p. 259). I find these sweeping generalizations about progressive education and an unqualified endorsement of the standards movement puzzling to say the least.

Frances Vaughan

Frances Vaughan is a psychotherapist who has written extensively on transpersonal issues. For example, she has written a book that deals extensively with the transpersonal self (Vaughan, 1986). She argues, like Wilber, that there are several levels of existence – physical, emotional, mental, existential, and spiritual – and that we have identities associated with each level. The transpersonal self is linked with the spiritual level. Vaughan draws the following distinction between the transpersonal self and the super-ego:

Super-Ego	Transpersonal Self
Judgmental	Compassionate
Fearful	Loving
Opinionated	Wise
Intrusive	Receptive
Dominating	Allowing
Limited	Unlimited
Rationalizing	Intuitive
Controlled	Spontaneous
Restrictive	Creative
Conventional	Inspired
Anxious	Peaceful
Defensive	Open
Separated	Connected (pp. 42–3)

Vaughan suggests that the transpersonal self can be accessed through disidentification with the ego, meditation, and visualization. She suggests the following exercise to realize the self, which provides an appropriate conclusion to this chapter:

Dialogues with the Transpersonal Self

Each of us has within us a source of wisdom, compassion, and creativity that we can learn to contact.

Imagine that your transpersonal Self represents the highest qualities that you value. This image of your Self embodies all the positive qualities that are latent within you and that you might expect to find in an enlightened being. It embodies your intuitive knowing, your inner wisdom, and your loving kindness. If you were to visibly embody these qualities, how would you see yourself?

Let the image go now, and focus attention on your breathing. When your mind is quiet and your body relaxed, imagine that you are walking alone in a beautiful place where you feel perfectly safe. Reflect on your life as it is and consider any problem that may be troubling you. Pick one issue that you are concerned about and formulate a single question on which you would like to receive guidance.

Imagine now that your transpersonal Self has come to meet you where you are. Take a moment to imagine what it feels like to be in the presence of a being of total compassion. You can ask this being whatever you want to know. Whatever answer is given, listen and take time to reflect on it.

It may be exactly what you need to know for the next step on your way. Trust your Self. Become your Self. Let go, say goodbye, and return to being here now in your ordinary waking state. (pp. 56–7)

Conclusion

The focus in this chapter has been on the unconditioned self or soul. The latter part of this book will focus on some strategies that nourish this part of ourselves. However, the holistic curriculum attempts to facilitate the development of the whole person including the ego. One way of seeing life is as a dance between our ego and soul. We want to support a healthy ego that can manage our daily affairs and social relations. It is also important that we acknowledge what Carl Jung called the 'shadow' or darker aspects of our psyche. The self can help witness and ultimately accept our shadow and all aspects of ourselves. Simply put, it can help us be whole.

References

Assagioli, R. (1965). *Psychosynthesis*. New York: Viking.

Esbjorn-Hargens, S. (in press, 2005). Integral by design: How integral theory informs teaching, learning and curriculum in a graduate program. *Revision 28.*

Ferrer, J.N. (2002). *Revisioning transpersonal theory: A participatory vision of human spirituality*. Albany, NY: SUNY Press.

Ferrucci, P. (1982). *What we may be*. Los Angeles, CA: Tarcher.

Gardner, H. (1983). *Frames of mind*. New York: Basic Books.

Hart, T. (2002). Truth, values, and decompressing data: Seeing information as living words. *Encounter: Education for Meaning and Social Justice, 15*(1), 4–10.

Hoffman, E. (1980). The Kabbalah. *Journal of Humanistic Psychology, 20*, 33–47.

Johnson, C. (ed.). (1971). *Vedanta: An anthology of Hindu scripture, commentary and poetry*. New York: Bantam.

Jung, C. (1933). *Modern man in search of a soul*. New York: Harcourt, Brace and World.

Jung, C. (1968). *Man and his symbols*. Garden City, NY: Doubleday.

Knudston, P., & Suzuki, D. (1992). *Wisdom of the elders*. Toronto: Stoddart.

Marshak, D. (1997). *The common vision: Parenting and educating for wholeness*. New York: Peter Lang.

McNamara, W. (1975). Psychology and the Christian mystical tradition. In C. Tart (Ed.), *Transpersonal Psychologies* (pp. 395–436). New York: Harper and Row.

Merton, T. (1959). *The inner experience.* Unpublished manuscript.

Samuels, M., & Samuels, N. (1975). *Seeing with the mind's eye.* New York: Random House.

Scholem, G.G. (1961). *Major trends in Jewish mysticism.* New York: Schochen.

Shah, I. (1970). *Tales of the dervishes.* New York: Dutton.

Shah, I. (1971). *The dermis probe.* New York: Dutton.

Suzuki, D. (ed.) (1956). W. Barrett. *Zen Buddhism.* Garden City, NY: Doubleday.

Trungpa, C. (1984). *Shambhala: The sacred path of the warrior.* Boston: Shambhala.

Vaughan, F. (1986). *The inward arc: Healing and wholeness in psychotherapy and spirituality.* Boston: Shambhala.

Wilber, K. (1980). *The Atman project.* Wheaton, IL: Theosophical Publishing House.

Wilber, K. (1983). *A sociable God.* New York: McGraw-Hill.

Wilber, K. (1995). *Sex, ecology and spirituality: The evolution of spirit.* Boston: Shambhala.

Wilber, K. (1997). *The eye of the spirit: An integral vision for a world gone slightly mad.* Boston: Shambhala.

Wilber, K. (1999). *One taste: The journals of Ken Wilber.* Boston: Shambhala.

CHAPTER FOUR

The Social Context: An Ecological / Interdependent Perspective

We have tended to think non-contextually in terms of education; that is, we have not linked the school curriculum to the surrounding social milieu. One of the assumptions of this book is that a particular curriculum approach can often be linked with a parallel social context. With regard to the three positions of learning, the following links can be made:

1. transmission position – laissez-faire economics
2. transaction position – rational planning
3. transformation position – an ecological approach

In this chapter, I would like to briefly refer to the first two positions and then outline the transformation perspective in more detail.

Transmission Position – Laissez-Faire Economics

Atomistic economics is based on Adam Smith's laissez-faire approach in which individuals compete in the marketplace. The market is the regulating mechanism for setting the price and quality of goods. Heilbroner (1980) has described the atomistic world of Smith:

> The world of Adam Smith has been called a world of atomistic competition; a world in which no agent of the productive mechanism, on the side of labor or capital, was powerful enough to interfere with or to resist the pressures of competition. It was a world in which each agent was forced to scurry after its self-interest in a vast social free-for-all. (p. 56)

Milton Friedman (Friedman & Friedman, 1980) picked up the banner of Smith when he claimed, 'In its simplest form, such a society consists of a number of independent households – a collection of Robinson Crusoes, as it were' (p. 13). For Friedman the principal link for these individuals is the marketplace. Friedman argues that 'the key insight of Adam Smith's *Wealth of Nations* is misleadingly simple: if an exchange between two parties is voluntary, it will not take place unless both believe they will benefit from it' (Friedman & Friedman, 1980, p. 13). One of the problems with this perspective is that it divorces or fragments economic activity from the rest of life and has made it easy for the capitalist to ignore the social and ecological costs of his or her economic activity. When economic activity is reduced to individual self-interest and competition, then it is easy to excuse the dumping of toxins into rivers or the use of abusive labour practices.

Laissez-faire approaches have led to excessive individualism, particularly in the United States. Individualism has promoted fragmentation as there is little attempt to define the common good, much less work towards such a goal. Bellah (1986) has explored this problem in his work.

Transaction Position – Rational Planning

The transaction position is based on the assumption that humans can rationally intervene to improve their affairs. Particularly helpful in this intervention process is the scientific method. John Dewey believed that the social sciences had progressed to the point where people could make 'intelligence and ideas the supreme force for the settlement of social issues' (as cited in Morris, 1986). Pragmatists influenced the growth of social improvement schemes, particularly city planning. For example, Robert Park, a contemporary of Dewey's at the University of Chicago, believed that one could control the physical environment of the city so that the people would experience better physical and mental health. Charles Morris (1986) believes that Dewey and Park were forerunners of the social engineering that pervaded the Kennedy–Johnson years of the 1960s:

The social-engineering bias was identical in its rationalist premises to the concepts of Lyndon Johnson's Great Society forty years later. Society was like a machine. With enough research, you could understand how the parts fit together – 'model' it, in latter-day jargon – then, by adroitly manipulating the social inputs, you would produce predictable improvements in the outputs: people would be healthier, friendlier, more industrious. (p. 10)

In the early 1960s social engineering seemed to work. The economy boomed with low inflation, and the social programs during the early Johnson years were carried out with great enthusiasm. Social engineering was applied to foreign affairs in the form of U.S. intervention in Vietnam. Here the assumptions of pragmatism and social engineering began to founder. The Vietnamese resistance to American force was much greater than the technocrats had predicted. Both the tactical and moral failure of the Vietnamese adventure contributed greatly to the counterculture and planted the seeds of present-day transformational perspectives. Paul Warnke, upon leaving the Pentagon in 1969, stated that the problem with the North Vietnamese was that they did not behave like reasonable people (Morris, 1986). The rationalist model can never fully anticipate how an individual or a group of individuals will act. The more recent experience of American military intervention in Iraq is further evidence of how such rational planning can go awry.

Not only did rational planning and intervention break down in Vietnam, it also foundered in economics. Ever since the 1930s, governments had tended to rely on Keynesian theory, which used deficit spending to stimulate the economy. However, inflation in the 1970s eroded the Keynesian consensus. Supply-side economics replaced belief in government intervention to stimulate the economy. In general, 'New Deal' liberals became discredited and liberalism searched for alternatives, particularly those associated with new technologies.

Yet the faith in technology holds the same difficulties as the belief in rational planning. Sale (1980) calls this belief in technology 'technofix.' As an example of technofix thinking he cites former Atomic Energy Commission Chairman Glenn T. Seaborg, who said, 'We must pursue the idea, that it is more science, better science, more wisely applied that is going to free us from (our) predicaments ... and to set the underlying philosophy for a rationale for the future handling of our technological and social development' (p. 35). The technofix solution for anxiety is Valium, and for the oil shortage it is coal liquefaction. The limitations of technology continue to alarm us, however. In 1986 the Shuttle disaster and the meltdown at Chernobyl reminded us that technologies are only as good as the bureaucracies that run them. In short, technology does not operate in a socio-political vacuum. Only when we begin to look at problems in a connected, holistic way can we move beyond the fragmentation of laissez-faire thinking and the naivety of technofix.

Transformation Position – An Interdependent Perspective

An interdependent perspective regarding social-economic-political thinking starts with the assumption that all human activity is interconnected and, thus, a change introduced in one area can have effects in other areas. This approach is based on several principles:

1. an ecological sense
2. human-scale organizations
3. non-violent change
4. androgyny

An Ecological Sense

An ecological sense starts with the premise that human life is only part of a much larger fabric that includes plants, animals, and the entire biosphere in which we live. We have many examples of how humans, both today and in the past, have ignored this ecological awareness. One example comes from the Roman empire, which overharvested the lands around the Mediterranean to feed its large urban populations. The farming techniques led to a runoff of topsoil and eventually the desertification of much of the land, particularly in North Africa. It was the Roman empire's lack of ecological sense that was mainly responsible for the Sahara Desert.

Today, of course, erosion continues to occur around the world. In the United States, the Army Corps of Engineers reported in 1978 that nearly half of the continental U.S. coastline was suffering from severe erosion with about 21 per cent of the coastline classified as 'critical' (Sale, 1980). We are often guilty of ecological hubris in that we continue to ignore the ecological context and often suffer as a result. For example, developers continue to build homes on the hills around Los Angeles despite evidence that continued building robs the soil of its absorbent cover. Thus, the soil continues to erode and leads to millions of dollars of damage when, with high rainfall, homes are destroyed by mudslides. The following letter to the *New York Times* in 1978 expresses ecological hubris very well:

To the Editor:

According to all the Judeo-Christian religions, as expressed in the biblical word which they all accept as divinely authoritative, God gave man, made in His image and likeness, dominion over all the earth and its hosts. Then why must we tolerate being subjected to the wild caprices of unstable air masses, including the ultimate obscenity called the tornado, in which a wayward, rapidly rotating air funnel deals death and destruction with impunity to whatever happens to lie in its path?

Why don't the world's leading scientific minds and its political leaders, starting here in this country and possibly operating through the United Nations, give top priority to subjugating the earth's atmosphere, making it totally and abjectly responsive to the well-being and security not of mankind alone but of all life on earth, as well as the solid structures and tools of man's devising?

My blood boils every time I read that a high wind or the pressure gradient in an air mass constituting a tornado kills people, wrecks buildings, tosses cars around like playthings, etc., often as not without the slightest warning. Let us have 'weather by the consent of the weathered' and force the elements to respect our wishes! (as cited in Sale, 1980, p. 15)

A few months later, the Federal Weather Modification Advisory Board suggested that in twenty years they would be able to control the weather over much of the country. The attempt to control weather is probably the height of our hubris, as thirty years later we can hardly predict the weather much less control it.

There have been significant improvements in our relationship to the environment. Gregg Easterbrook (2003) documents these changes particularly with regard to cleaner water and air in North America and Europe. Easterbrook does acknowledge, however, the global problem of greenhouse-gas accumulation as the main environmental challenge of our time.

What are examples of an ecological sense? Of course, nature itself provides many examples. Fritjof Capra (1982, p. 281) has described the interconnections in the form of a diagram (see figure 4.1). In a later work Capra (1996) elaborates on the concept of network, which is central to an ecological perspective:

The web of life consists of networks within networks. At each scale, under closer scrutiny, the nodes of the network reveal themselves as smaller

Figure 4.1 An Ecological Sense

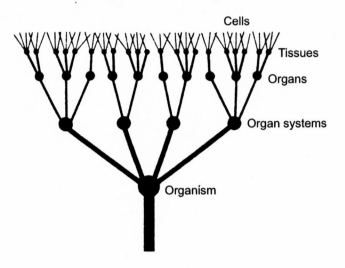

networks ... In nature there is no 'above' or 'below,' and there are no hierarchies. There are only networks nesting within networks.

During the last few decades the network perspectives has become more
and more central to ecology. As the ecologist Bernard Patten put it in his
concluding remarks to a recent conference on ecological networks: 'Ecology is networks ... To understand ecosystems ultimately will be to understand networks.' (p. 35)

According to Capra (1982), nature is composed of interconnected
systems that form multilevel structures. At each level are 'integrated,
self-organizing wholes consisting of smaller parts and at the same time,
acting as parts of larger wholes' (p. 280). A human being is an organism that is made up of organ systems (e.g., respiratory system), which
are composed of organs (e.g., the lungs), which are composed of tissue
(lung tissue), which is, in turn, composed of cells. However, each of
these levels is a subsystem. Arthur Koestler described such a subsystem as a 'holon' that has both independent properties of a whole and
related properties because it is part of a system. In this context, it is possible to view the universe as a related set of minds: 'individual human
minds are embedded in the larger minds of social and ecological sys-

tems, and these are integrated into the planetary mental system – the mind of Gaia – which in turn must participate in some kind of universal or cosmic mind' (as cited in Capra, 1982, p. 292).

BIOREGIONS

One example of networks at an ecological and geographical level is the *bioregion*. Thomas Berry (1988) has proposed that human activity be grounded in biological regions such as river valleys, plains, mountain ranges, and other natural geographic areas. Berry states that each bioregion 'is coherent within itself and intimately related to others. Together they express the wonder of this garden planet of the universe' (pp. 163–4). Human beings need to see themselves in this localized context where they are woven into the ongoing processes of nature.

Berry argues that there are six main functions of the bioregion. First is *self-propagation*, which requires that humans recognize and respect the rights of each species living within the region. The second function is *self-nourishment*, which means that members of the community sustain one another. This function refers to commercial and economic activity that should be modelled on the natural world, which is much more economical with regard to how it deals with waste. The third function is *'self-education* through physical, chemical, biological, and cultural patterning' (p. 167). From this perspective evolution is seen as a self-educational process as the earth and each of its bioregions has 'performed unnumbered billions of experiments in designing the existing life system'(p. 167). *Self-governance* is the fourth function of bioregions. Each region should be able to look after it own affairs through participatory activity. The fifth function is *self-healing*. Bioregions experience natural disasters such as flooding and earthquakes but have the capability of regenerating themselves. Berry notes that humans can find healing through submission to the earth community and acceptance of its natural healing powers. Finally, *self-fulfilling activities* are another function of the bioregion. These happen 'in religious liturgies, in market festivals, in the solemnities of political assembly, in all manner of play, in music and dance, in all the visual and performing arts. From these come the cultural identity of the bioregion' (p. 168).

Sale (1980) states that the use of solar energy reflects an ecological sense and is congruent with Berry's vision of the bioregion. First, it does not pollute and is a quiet, odour-free form of energy. It does not use fossil fuels and thus conserves nature's resources. It is also suited to small-scale operations and can be controlled by the people who use it. The sun's energy cannot be monopolized by a few energy companies. For example, in 1979 a thousand separate firms were engaged in the solar energy business (Sale, 1980). Solar energy is also very flexible: a solar unit can be constructed in a matter of days or weeks, while a nuclear power plant takes several years or even decades to plan and build. Solar energy is efficient in that very little energy is lost through conversion and transmission. This is in contrast to the usual sources of energy used by electrical utilities in which 50–65 per cent of the original energy is lost through conversion and transmission. The technology associated with solar energy is relatively simple and does not require complex delivery systems or large storage capacities. Finally, solar energy is adaptable to any sort of thermodynamic job. Water can be easily heated to be used for hot water, electrical generation, or even for steel manufacturing. In contrast, nuclear energy requires that uranium reach 2400 degrees F and then all the heat has to be drained away to heat a house at 70 degrees F, an incredibly inefficient process. Of course, the question arises, Why has solar energy not become more widely used? This question of use raises the problem that in industrialized countries large, powerful structures (electrical utilities and oil companies) have a vested interest in the present forms of energy. To expand the use of solar energy, one must examine it as a part of a larger process of moving toward what Sale (1980) calls a 'human scale society.' The high price of oil in the twenty-first century has substantially increased interest in alternative energy sources such solar and wind power.

As mentioned earlier, the model for an ecological sense comes from nature itself. Nature can be a reminder of the connectedness of all beings, as in Lewis Thomas's (1975) discussion of the bacteria in his body:

> There they are, moving about in my cytoplasm ... They are much less closely related to me than to each other and to the free-living bacteria out under the hill. They feel like strangers, but the thought comes that the same creatures, precisely the same, are out there in the cells of seagulls, and whales, and dune grass, and seaweed and hermit crabs, and further inland in the leaves of the beech in my backyard, and in the family of skunks beneath the back fence, and even in that fly on the window. Through them, I am connected: I have close relatives, once removed, all over the place. (p. 86)

Human-Scale Organizations

Kirkpatrick Sale's book entitled *Human Scale* describes how human beings need to live and work in organizations that are reasonable in size. 'Man is the measure' has been the guide for centuries. Sale (1980) claims:

> Was that not the explicitly stated principle of Pericles, of Leonardo, of Jefferson, of Corbusier, and hundreds of others of our most capable planners and thinkers? Indeed, is it not the essential spirit within Jewish mythology, Christian ethics, Anglo-Saxon law, Renaissance humanism, Protestant separatism, merchant capitalism, the French Revolution, the American Republic, Marxism, Darwinism, Freudianism, of so many of the basic currents – though by no means all, of course – of Western history? So in any search for a desirable future, for the ways in which tools, buildings, communities, cities, shops, offices, factories, meeting places, forums, and legislatures should be constructed, I see no reason to go beyond this simple rule: they should all be built to human scale. (p. 37)

Human scale describes buildings that do not dwarf the individual or the surroundings. Human scale means that buildings allow the natural world to co-exist with the human-made world. Sale, however, feels that human scale can be applied to economics, health care, education, and, in fact, most areas of human activity. Sale cites several examples of human-scale communities: the solar-powered community of Davis, California; the Quaker meeting; the communes in Israel; the town meetings in New England communities; and the restructuring of many corporations along non-authoritarian lines.

The central values of human scale include individual fulfillment, community cooperation, harmony with nature, decentralization of power, and self-sufficiency. Sale believes that a number of trends in today's society support the move to human scale. These include the consumer movement; the back-to-nature spirit that prompted a threefold increase in visits to national parks from 1960 to 1978; the so-called 'underground economy' that operates outside of the standard marketplace and allows people to barter and trade services; the cooperative movement that includes credit unions, health co-ops, food co-ops, and electricity co-ops; and the do-it-yourself movement (Sale, 1980).

Our modern cities are good examples of environments that are not built to human scale. In particular, the skyscraper does not let us view the building as a whole but dominates the landscape in an almost forbidding manner. One could hypothesize that the rootlessness of modern city living is exacerbated by high-rise apartment and office buildings. If one lives in a high-rise apartment and then works in a high-rise office, the only contact with the earth may be the short walk on the concrete sidewalk to the subway. The city inhabitant, then, never feels that he or she is part of an organic environment.

One of the principal examples of human-scale living is the village. Richard Critchfield (1983) points out that villages have been one of the central features of human life for centuries. According to Sale (1980) anthropological evidence suggests that the oldest human institution is not the family but the village or tribe. The family has usually been a subunit in a somewhat larger community. This larger community – the tribe or village – was the source of language and culture. There is evidence that once the village or tribe reached over 5000 or 6000 people, it became too complex and had to either self-destruct or readjust (Sale, 1980).

Critchfield lived in villages around the world for a quarter of a century. Although he criticizes some aspects of village life (e.g., male domination), many aspects represent a form of life that is integrated and organic. For example, village residents usually feel closely tied to the land. Villagers' morale is often high when they are harvesting and working hard but tends to fall during periods of idleness.

Village morality is linked with working on the land and encourages monogamous, divorceless, multi-child marriages. In brief, villagers believe in hard work and a moral code that provides a sense of continuity. However, the villager tends to be sceptical of formal religion; instead, they have a strong personal faith in a God that watches over their personal welfare. In general, the villager lives in a world fused with meaning. Critchfield makes the point that all of the world's great religions come from villages. According to Critchfield (1983),

> the Western political ideologies of nationalism, socialism, communism, capitalism and democracy have all emerged in cities. No great religion ever has. Abraham was a herdsman, Zoroaster raised cattle, Jesus was a village carpenter's son, Mohammed a shepherd and later a petty trader and Buddha, though a Hindu prince, came from a remote backwater of Nepal. These religions were all formed as little village traditions in revolt against existing city traditions which had somehow failed millions of villagers, just as the Westernization of the great Third World cities so often fails them now. They all emerged in civilizations which, like ours, were in extremis. Prophets come from villages. (p. 234)

Critchfield does see a number of changes occurring in villages around the world. Technology is being applied to farming methods, contraception is being widely practised, and the role of women is gradually changing in some villages. In his almost twenty-five years of travel in the villages of the Third World, however, Critchfield has become more concerned about the future of the West. At the conclusion of his book, Critchfield argues for a synthesis of village life with the technological progress of the West:

> The years in the villages have been enough to persuade me that a good many of these people are going to make it and that along the way they'll have lots to tell us. Our lives are not meant to be perpetually fun, self-absorbed Carnavals, reaching for the fast buck and getting zonked out on consumer goodies; that way, when the party's over, you can end up in the kicked-in-the-ribs purgatory of the emergency room. Nor are they meant to be one long back-breaking drudgery over a hoe or a plow.
>
> Certainly, we, with all our technology, wealth and freedom of individual choice, and they, with their closeness to nature and the self-responsibility that comes with living in groups, can come up with something a little better, a way to live that combines the best of our material goods with their simplicity and truth.
>
> We're not all villagers. But our grandfathers were. And so our grandchildren may become. In this book I've made many us-and-them distinctions. But I'll bet you've discovered little about these villagers that you don't recognize. Go to a village and you can't go too far wrong if you assume that everybody is just like you. For in the largest sense, and in those human qualities that really count, on this rather small planet there is only one big us. (p. 338)

Many people, of course, cannot move to a smaller community. However, they can adopt a slower lifestyle. Carol Honore (2004) has written about what he calls a 'worldwide movement that is challenging the cult of speed.' This movement has its roots in the slow food movement, which began in Italy as an alternative to fast food, and has spread to other areas of life including medicine, work, education, sex, and leisure. There is now even a 'slow city' in Italy, which in its founding manifesto declared: 'A firm defense of quiet material pleasure is the only way to oppose the universal folly of Fast Life' (as cited in Holt, 2002, p. 266).

Like holistic education, slow education is opposed to the mechanical product orientation of standards-led school reform. Maurice Holt (2002) suggests that the accountability movement creates 'a system of schools geared solely to the product-test results – and not to the process of creating educative experiences.' He concludes: 'The result of creating fast schools is institutional indigestion, and signs of discomfort are now appearing' where 'courses crammed in too much material at the expense of understanding' (p. 268).

In contrast, slow education encourages students to pursue questions in depth and not skip quickly through a curriculum of unrelated facts. Holt suggests:

> One takes time to see what Newton's concepts of mass and force might imply, to appreciate their abstract nature and the intellectual leap they represent. Then the usual algorithms fall into place quickly and securely. The slow school offers the intellectual space for scrutiny, argument and resolution. (p. 269)

Holt believes that the increase of home-schooled children is also a form of slow education that has a more flexible approach to learning. When our attitude to teaching and learning slows down, students can have moments when time stops and they experience timeless learning. Many spiritual teachers have encouraged the spiritual practitioner to 'slow down.' Eknath Easwaran (1989) has written about what he calls 'hurry sickness' in our society, which can be countered with patience and slowing down. David Elkind (1989) wrote about the 'hurried child,' whose days are constantly crammed with planned activities. He calls for a more relaxed childhood that is congruent with the slow school movement.

Sale also argues for human-scale educational institutions. He refers to research done by Barker and Gump (1964) that studied school size and its effects on education. Barker and his colleagues spent three years studying thirteen high schools in eastern Kansas, ranging in size from 40 to 2000 students. The study focused on how size was related to student participation in athletics, class discussion, and extracurricular activities. In such activities as music, drama, journalism, and student government, participation was highest in the schools with enrollments between 61 and 150. With regard to classroom activities, while the bigger school offered more subjects, the students in the larger schools participated in fewer and less varied classes than the students in smaller schools. In the music classes, which were studied in detail, Barker and Gump found that musical education and experience were more widely distributed in the small school.

Further research supports the finding that students in small schools do better academically (Cotton, 1996; Lee & Smith, 1994; Wasley, 2000). In reviewing studies that examine different institutions dealing with children, the World Health Organization (WHO) concludes that institutions should be no larger than one hundred children. According to WHO, when organizations are larger than this, informal discipline based on personal contact is replaced by impersonal, institutional authority (Sale, 1980).

Research also shows that small schools do not cost more to operate than large schools and may, in fact, be more cost-effective with savings in remediation (Gregory, 1992). Collegial professional relationships that are important to effective schooling are also facilitated in small schools (Ark, 2002). Finally, a recent report of the National Center for Education Statistics (1999) documents that small schools are safer than large schools. Large schools are eight times more likely to report a serious violent incident than small schools. Students are more anonymous in large schools, which also tend to rely on security measures such as metal detectors. Klonsky (2002) concludes that many of the new small-by-design schools share important attributes: personalization, high student visibility, and the close collaboration of teachers.

If human scale is the measure for our institutions, what are the means of helping us to arrive there? One alternative is a non-violent approach to change.

Non-Violent Change

The tenets of non-violence have been articulated by Thoreau, Tolstoy, Gandhi, and Martin Luther King. Non-violent change is based on the principle that one's opponent should be not objectified. Erikson (1969) discusses this in *Gandhi's Truth,* which is about the strike at the textile factory in Ahmedabad, where Ghandi represented the workers. Gandhi never reduced his opponents, the mill owners, to objects of hate and condemnation. In Erikson's terms, he always left room in the encounter so that a degree of mutuality might develop between the opponents.

Central to the notion of change is respect for the person's individual conscience. Thoreau, in particular, believed that morality should rest on personal conscience. In his famous essay *Civil Disobedience* Thoreau (1986) argues for resistance to unjust laws and governments through non-participation and non-cooperation. Non-violence does not mean passivity. Thoreau calls for non-payment of taxes that support war and slavery. Thoreau also suggests that, in an unjust society, the appropriate place for the just person may be jail. This idea was adopted by Gandhi and King in their protests. Richardson (1986) connects this strand in Thoreau's thinking to Stoicism, noting that Ellery Channing, Thoreau's contemporary, said that Thoreau was a natural Stoic. Stoicism contains many of the principles of holism. The Roman Stoic Marcus Aurelius (1964) said, 'Always think of the universe as one living organism, with a single substance and a single soul ... there is a law that governs the course of nature and should govern human actions' (p. 73). Richardson claims that 'in contrast to Epicureanism, which held that the universe is made up of atoms and empty space, the Stoics held that God is immanent in all created things but has no separate existence outside them' (p. 190). The Stoics believed strongly in the individual and in personal conscience. Thoreau was able to link his concern for the individual with his love of nature. Richardson (1986) states:

> Thoreau is probably the greatest spokesman of the last two hundred years for the view that we must turn not to the state, not to a God, and not to society, but to nature for our morality. He stands as the most attractive American example as Emerson was the great proponent of the ageless Stoic principle of self-trust, self-reverence, or self-reliance, as it is variously called. Thoreau's life can be thought of as one long uninterrupted attempt to work out the practical concrete meaning of the Stoic idea that the laws ruling nature rule men as well. (p. 191)

Related to the issue of non-violence is reverence for life. It is difficult to injure a living thing if one sees all life as part of a connected whole. How can you injure someone when you see the person as part of yourself?

In contrast to Marxism, non-violent change is more organically connected to one's inner being. The goal in non-violent change is not just to reform society with more appropriate laws and institutions but to seek more fundamental change within the person. So often, political revolution has often replaced one form of repression (right-wing dictatorship) with another form (totalitarian communism). One type of elite replaces another. People often try to become 'good Marxists,' and thus they give up their own subjectivity; in other words, they adopt a social role rather than listening to the deeper part of themselves. This problem is also apparent in so-called 'New Age' movements, as people try to conform to some ideal (e.g., the good Waldorfian).

From a holistic perspective it is important to work from the inside out (Hunt, 1987). Change, then, should be congruent with our centre, not with some external set of expectations. King and Gandhi were able to reach the deepest part of the person and thus bring about non-exploitative change.

Androgyny

As we contact our soul, we become more whole. This means that we let go of roles for which we have been conditioned – for example, sexual roles. Androgyny means that we no longer think of ourselves as exclusively masculine or feminine; instead we can begin to see ourselves as whole people made up of opposites, or polarities. This does not mean that men must necessarily become more sensitive or emotional; it only means that we can awaken to the polarities that are within us. Feminine and masculine can be viewed in relation to polarities such as:

yin	yang
intuitive	rational
holistic	analytic
responsive	initiating
nurturing	achieving
contracting	expanding

From our centre we can open to and work with these polarities rather than getting caught up in one set of qualities. If we get caught up in one polarity, we close ourselves off to part of our own being. Research indicates that people who are able to integrate these polarities are more able to comprehend ambiguous information and deal with the coexistence of incongruous qualities within one person (Halverson, 1970; Tripoldi & Bieri, 1966) and are more able to change (Delia, Crockett & Gonyea, 1970). A number of psychologists, such as Erikson, Jung, Singer, and Maslow, have also claimed that the ability to accept and then integrate the different parts of oneself is a sign of psychological growth. For example, Maslow (1942) found that self-actualizing men and women are similar in their transcendence of traditional male and female stereotypes.

Despite this acceptance of polarities by certain psychologists, in the West we have tended to accept one set of qualities (masculine–yang) as desirable, and the other set (feminine–yin) as less desirable. In contrast, the Eastern approach is to see the polarities as related to one another and as part of a larger whole. Either/or conceptualization is problematic in that it forces us to accept a limited identity. According to Olds (1981), working with both polarities can move us to higher levels of consciousness:

> Often the mode of liberation comes precisely through the heightening of tension between two incompatible modes of thought or concepts. The leverage point for new alternatives of thought or action lies in the posing of paradox and the simultaneous existence of two incompatible thoughts or commands. This is the method of Zen (Suzuki, 1964) and of the Yaqui sorcerer in Castaneda's (1968, 1971) writings who helps him break through the interpretive webs he confuses with reality by flowing back and forth between discrepant, alternative world views and learning to 'see.' Thus wholeness, synthesis, and the transcending of polarity seem to characterize the human ideal in philosophic speculation as well as in psychological health. (p. 19)

Androgyny is another metaphor for wholeness. The word is derived from the Greek *andros* (man) and *gyne* (woman). June Singer (1976), working from a Jungian framework, has been one of the main proponents of androgyny as a metaphor for wholeness and she sees it as a rediscovered archetype and inner guide. It is also possible to see androgyny as a cultural and social norm rather than as a purely psychological term. For example, Bem (1972, 1974, 1975) has focused on androgyny as a social norm that can promote a less exploitive society. From this perspective androgyny is not limited to the struggle for equal rights for women. Its broader aim is to balance our Western emphasis on technology, competitiveness, individualism, and logical thinking with the feminine values of nurturing cooperation, relatedness, and love. Olds (1981) sees the restoration of feminine values as a vehicle for a broad cultural synthesis:

> The ultimate form of revolution, in fact, might be a kind of revolution in consciousness and spirituality involving the transcendence of duality and dichotomous thinking in all spheres, unleashing tremendous cultural crossbreeding, synthesis, and integration. The revaluation of the feminine mode of consciousness as part of an androgynous goal augurs well for both scientific renewal and spiritual evolution, broadening the parameters of each pursuit and enlarging the scope of our inquiry. (p. 245)

There is a danger, however, of being too rigid in our ideal of androgyny. Instead, it is more useful to view it as a metaphor. If we define too limited an ideal, then people will feel a need to conform to this ideal and feel guilty if they do not live up to it. Thus, the woman who stresses caring as a principle focus for her life might feel uneasy if she were working, and the man who works long hours might become guilty about not spending enough time at home. Again, we need to turn to our centre as a guide in working with inner polarities.

Summary

The social context for the holistic curriculum focuses on an environment that values wholeness and where people can interact in human-scale communities. The following chart summarizes the characteristics of social contexts associated with each of the three positions of learning.

Transmission	Transaction	Transformation
laissez-faire	rational planning	economic activity linked to ecological awareness
conservative	liberal	transcending traditional polarities
competition	regulated competition	cooperation/regulated competition
big business tends to dominate marketplace	big business and big government dominate	human scale economies
decisions based on profit/loss	centralized decision making, often by bureaucracy	decentralized decision making that includes social and ecological costs
nature and economic activity viewed as separate	nature and economic activity linked through rational planning	nature and economic activity seen as interconnected

hard data	quantitative data used (e.g., mathematical models)	emphasis on quality; hard and soft data integrated
human needs determined by marketplace/ advertising	needs influenced by rational planning	needs viewed organically; appropriate consumption
individual roles linked to market (e.g., specialization)	roles linked to liberal, democratic fulfillment theory (e.g., inalienable rights)	roles linked to connection to community
narrow sex roles	flexible roles linked to equal rights legislation	androgyny/transcending sex roles
change determined by market fluctuations	rational/planned change	non-violent change responding to inner needs
short-term view	longer-term view linked to planning	evolutionary, organic view of change
top-down organizations	democratic organizations; rational consensus	consensus includes awareness of spiritual and emotional needs

References

Ark, T.V. (2002). The case for small schools. *Education Leadership, 59*, 55–9.

Aurelius, Marcus. (1964). *Meditations*. New York: Penguin.

Barker, R.B., & Gump, P.V. (1964). *Big school, small school*. Palo Alto, CA: Stanford University Press.

Bellah, R.N. (1986). *Habits of the heart: Individualism and commitment in American life*. New York: Harper & Row.

Bem, S.L. (1972). *Psychology looks at sex roles: Where have all the androgynous people gone?* Paper presented at UCLA Symposium on Women, Los Angeles, CA.

Bem, S.L. (1974). The measurement of psychological androgyny. *Journal of Consulting and Clinical Psychology, 42*, 155–62.

Bem, S.L. (1975). Androgyny vs. the tight little lives of fluffy women and chesty men. *Psychology Today, 9*, 58–62.

Berry, T. (1988). *The dream of the earth.* San Francisco, CA: Sierra Club Books.

Capra, F. (1982). *The turning point.* New York: Simon & Schuster.

Capra, F. (1996). *The web of life: A new scientific understanding of living systems.* New York: Anchor.

Cotton, K. (1996). *Close-up #20. School improvement research series.* Portland, OR: Northwest Regional Educational Lab.

Critchfield, R. (1983). *Villages.* Garden City, NY: Anchor Press/Doubleday.

Delia, J.G., Crockett, W.H., & Gonyea, A.H. (1970). Cognitive complexity and the effects of schemas on the learning of social structures. *Proceedings of the Annual Convention of the American Psychological Association, 5*, 373–4.

Easterbrook, G. (2003). *The paradox of progress: How life gets better while people feel worse.* New York: Random House.

Easwaran, E. (1989). *Original goodness: Strategies for uncovering your spiritual hidden resources.* Petaluma, CA: Nilgiri Press.

Elkind, D. (1989). *The hurried child.* Reading, MA: Addison Wesley.

Erikson, E. (1969). *Gandhi's truth.* New York: W.W. Norton.

Friedman, M., & Friedman, R. (1980). *Free to choose.* San Diego, CA: Harcourt, Brace, Jovanovich.

Gregory, T. (1992). Small is too big: Achieving a critical anti-mass in the high school. In *Source book on school and district size, cost and quality.* (pp. 1–31). Minneapolis: University of Minneapolis and Hubert H. Humphrey Institute of Public Affairs; Oak Brook, IL: North Central Regional Educational Laboratory.

Halverson, C.F. (1970). 'Interpersonal perception: Cognitive complexity and trait implication.' *Journal of Consulting and Clinical Psychology, 4*, 86–90.

Heilbroner, R.L. (1980). *The worldly philosophers.* New York: Touchstone Books.

Holt, M. (2002). It's time to start the slow school movement. *Phi Delta Kappan, 84*(4), 265–71.

Honore, C. (2004). *In praise of slowness: How a worldwide movement is challenging the cult of speed.* San Francisco: Harper.

Hunt, D.E. (1987). *Beginning with ourselves: In practice, theory and human affairs.* Toronto: OISE Press.

Klonsky, M. (2002). How smaller schools prevent school violence. *Educational Leadership, 59*, 65–70.

Lee. V., & Smith, J. (1994). *Effects of high school restructuring on size and achievement.* Madison, WI: National Center for Organization and Restructuring of Schools.

Maslow, A.H. (1942). 'Self esteem (dominance feeling) and sexuality in women.' *Journal of Social Psychology, 16*, 259–94.

Morris, C.R. (1986). *A time of passion: America 1960–80.* New York: Penguin Books.

National Center for Education Statistics. (1999). *Indicators of school crime and safety.* NCES 1999-057. Washington, DC: U.S. Department of Education, Office of Educational Research and Improvement.

Olds, L.E. (1981). *Fully human.* Englewood Cliffs, NJ: Prentice Hall.

Richardson, R.D. (1986). *Henry David Thoreau: A life of the mind.* Berkeley: University of California Press.

Sale, K. (1980). *Human scale.* New York: Perigee Books.

Singer, J. (1976). *Androgyny: Toward a new theory of sexuality.* Garden City, NY: Anchor Press/Doubleday.

Thomas, L. (1975). *The lives of a cell.* New York: Bantam.

Thoreau, H.D. (1986). *Walden and civil disobedience.* New York: Penguin Classics.

Tripoldi, T., & Bieri, J. (1966). Cognitive complexity, perceived conflict, and certainty. *Journal of Personality, 34,* 144–53.

Wasley, P. (2000). *Small schools and the issue of scale.* New York: Bank Street College of Education.

CHAPTER FIVE

Holistic Curriculum:
Historical Background

The holistic curriculum is not new. Educators and philosophers have articulated its principles and used it for centuries. However, each age has had to redefine the holistic curriculum in its own terms. The major problem confronting holistic educators has been integrating its two strands. One strand has focused on personal growth. Within this strand is a further division between those who stress psychological growth (humanistic educators) and those who emphasize spiritual growth (transpersonal educators). Of course, the line between these substrands is not always clear, as the transpersonal educators usually include psychological development as a component of spiritual growth.

The other strand has focused on social change. From this position educators have developed programs that encourage student involvement in the community. This involvement can take the form of service to the community or social action. The latter is somewhat more radical as the student tries to effect some change or improvement in the life of the community.

The holistic curriculum has been most effective when these strands have been integrated, as in the Modern School of New York and the work of Myles Horton.

Personal Growth Education

This section discusses educational approaches that have focused more on personal development than on social change.

The Greeks

Recent research (Hadot, 2002; McEvilley, 2002) suggests that Greek philosophers viewed philosophy not as a narrow intellectual endeavour but as a holistic, contemplative practice. Hadot states that the Platonic dialogues were not just an intellectual exercise but a form of spiritual practice that demanded self-inquiry and self-transformation. Hadot (2002) states: 'To live in a philosophical way meant, above all, to turn toward intellectual and spiritual life, carrying out a conversion which involved "the whole soul" – which is to say the whole of moral life' (p. 65).

Hadot describes various spiritual exercises that Greek philosophers pursued in their work; they practised various forms of contemplation such as being fully present in the moment. For example, the Roman poet and philosopher Horace wrote: 'Let the soul be happy in the present, and refuse to worry about what will come later ... Think about arranging the present as best you can, with serene mind. All else is carried away as by a river' (as cited in Hadot, 2002, p. 196).

Being in the present requires constant attention. This constant awareness was particularly stressed by the Stoics. Hadot notes:

> For them, philosophy was a unique act which had to be practiced at each instant, with constantly renewed attention (*proshoke*) to oneself and to the present moment ... Thanks to this attention, the philosopher is always perfectly aware not only of what he is doing, but also of what he is thinking (this is the task of lived logic) and of what he is – in other words, of his place within the cosmos. (p. 138)

Similarly, Buddhists practise mindfulness, which involves moment-to-moment awareness. Hadot makes the connection of Greek philosophy to ancient Asian philosophy when he cites his colleague Solere as saying that 'the ancients were perhaps closer to the Orient than we are' (as cited in Hadot, 2002, p. 279).

Important to both the Greeks and Indians was the *presence* of the teacher or guru. Hadot writes: 'Philosophy then becomes the lived experience of a presence. From the experience of the presence of a beloved being, we rise to the experience of a transcendent presence' (p. 70). This is similar to the concept of *darshan* in India, which involves being in the presence of an enlightened or realized person. Again this relationship between teacher and pupil is not just intellectual but is based on affection and love. According to Hadot the Greeks believed that even the study of science or geometry engages the entire soul and is 'always linked to Eros, desire, yearning, and choice' (p. 70).

Socrates' words 'know thyself' can be viewed as one of the first guidelines for holistic education. Socrates, with his relentless questioning, forced the individual to examine his or her own assumptions. Self-examination is based, in part, on the premise that all knowledge lies within and that we can discover it by contemplation. Socrates and Plato believed that the soul existed before birth and that by being put in a physical body it had forgotten its true identity. This is called the 'doctrine of reminiscence' (Ozman & Craver, 1981, p. 5). Socrates, then, acted as a midwife to draw out ideas that lay within the person. Plato, in the *Meno* dialogue, describes how Socrates extracted the Pythagorean theorem from a slave boy through inquiry. He drew out the theorem through a set of questions rather than telling him the theorem.

Plato described his approach to education in *The Republic*. He suggested a comprehensive educational system run by the state which would develop people to their full potential. Education, in Plato's view, should teach the person to see beyond the impermanence of the material world to intuit the 'real world' of ideas. Plato's allegory of the cave could also be seen as a metaphor for education. In this allegory prisoners are in darkness and in chains and they see only shadows on the walls of the cave. However, one of the prisoners walks up a steep slope and eventually into the sunlight. He realizes that he has been living in a world of illusion and returns to the cave to relate to his fellow prisoners his discovery. However, explaining his discovery involves risk because they may not believe that they are living in a world of shadows. Plato felt that the philosopher-teacher takes the risk and shares his or her knowledge with others. Thus, the teacher cannot remain in contemplation but must enter into the world and engage in dialogue with others.

Rousseau

One the most important historical figures in the humanist strand of holistic education is the French philosopher Jean Jacques Rousseau. In his book *Émile*, published in 1762, he described his approach to education. Rousseau advocated a natural approach to childrearing as he believed the natural soul of the child was good and must be protected from civilization. He said: 'From the outset raise a wall round your child's soul,' or it will be overcome by 'the crushing force of social conventions' (1955, p. 6). This romantic view of the child has continued to inspire humanistic and alternative school educators.

In *Émile*, Rousseau describes four stages of development – infancy, childhood, youth, and adulthood – corresponding to the four parts of the book. In the last part Rousseau describes his concept of negative education:

> Nature provides for the child's growth in her own way and this should never be thwarted. Do not make him sit still when he wants to run about, nor run when he wants to be quiet. If we did not spoil our children's wills by our blunders their desires would be free from caprice. (p. 50)

> Give him no orders at all, absolutely none. (p. 55)

> Give your scholar no verbal lessons, he should be taught by experience alone; never punish him, for he does not know what it is to do wrong; never make him say, 'Forgive me,' for he does not know how to do you wrong. Wholly unmoral in his actions, he can do nothing morally wrong, and he deserves neither punishment nor reproof. (p. 56)

> There the education of the earliest years should be merely negative. It consists, not in teaching virtue or truth, but in preserving the heart from vice and from the spirit of error. (p. 57)

Rousseau believed that the soul of the child was good and should be allowed to unfold according to its own natural pattern. The child, then, should be allowed to explore the world and make his or her own discoveries.

Of course, it is impossible to devise an education that is totally negative and unsupervised. There is, then, a contradiction within Rousseau's work and in the work of most romantic educators such as A.S. Neill. At one point Rousseau says, 'Take the opposite course with your pupil; let him always think he is master while you are really master ... No doubt he ought only do what he wants but he ought to want to do nothing but what you want him to do' (pp. 84–5). Here Rousseau describes the teacher as manipulator as he devises situations to seduce the child into learning. For example, Émile learns about measuring distance without instruments by playing games in the dark. Negative education, then, is not so easily practised and raises fundamental questions about the role of the teacher.

In a recent biography of Rousseau, Damrosch (2005) draws the following conclusion about *Émile*:

What was truly original was his claims that each person has a unique temperament that needs freedom to flourish ... His intention was to show how a person might prepare for life in society without sacrificing integrity, 'seeing with his own eyes, feeling with his own heart, and governed by no authority except his own reason.' (pp. 333–4)

Rousseau's phrase that the most useful rule in all of education is not 'to gain time but to lose it' has inspired many holistic educators such as George Dennison.

Pestalozzi and Froebel

Johann Heinrich Pestalozzi, the Swiss educator, was influenced by Rousseau, Locke, and Comenius, and thus his work shows both transactional and transformational influences. He also differs from Rousseau in that he taught most of his life and attempted to put his beliefs into practice. He cared about poor children and devoted much of his life to their education. Morf (as cited in de Guimps, 1889), summarizes the major principles of Pestalozzi's approach to education:

1. Intuition is the basis of instruction.
2. Language should be linked with intuition.
3. The time for learning is not the time for judgment and criticism.
4. In every branch, teaching should begin with the simplest elements and proceed gradually according to the development of the child, that is, in psychologically connected order.
5. Sufficient time should be devoted to each point of the teaching in order to ensure the complete mastery of it by the pupil.
6. Teaching should aim at development and not dogmatic exposition.
7. The educator should respect the individuality of the pupil.
8. The chief end of elementary teaching is not to impart knowledge and talent to the learner, but to develop and increase the powers of his intelligence.
9. Power must be linked to knowledge; and skill to learning.
10. The relations between the master and the pupil, especially as to discipline, should be based upon and ruled by love.
11. Instruction should be subordinated to the higher aim of education. (pp. 154–5)

Principles 7 and 10 reflect the influence of Rousseau. Many educational historians (Bayles & Hood, 1966) have argued that the real genius of Pestalozzi was his empathy for children and how he could adjust his instructional methods to the unique needs of each student. John Ramsauer, one of Pestalozzi's students, describes the informality of his classroom technique:

> There was no regular school plan nor order of lessons; and Pestalozzi did not limit himself to any fixed time, but often went on with the same subject for two or three hours. We numbered about sixty boys and girls from eight to fifteen years of age; our lessons lasted from eight o'clock in the morning till eleven; and in the afternoon from two o'clock till four, and the teaching was limited to drawing, arithmetic and exercises in language.
>
> There was neither reading nor writing; the pupils had no textbooks nor copy books and they learned nothing by heart. We had neither drawing models nor directions but slates only and red chalk, and whilst Pestalozzi made us repeat sentences about natural history as language exercises, we could draw whatever we liked; some drew little men and women; others houses; others again traced lines and arabesques according to their fancy. Pestalozzi never looked at what we drew or rather scribbled; but by the cuffs and elbows of our coats one could see that the scholars had made use of the red chalk. As for arithmetic we had between every two scholars a little frame divided into squares in which were points that we could count, add, multiply, subtract, and divide. (as cited in de Guimps, 1889, pp. 104–5)

Froebel was influenced by both Rousseau and Pestalozzi; however, his conception of education was more mystical. Froebel developed the kindergarten and focused on play as an important factor in the young child's development:

> Play is the first means of development of the human mind, its first effort to make acquaintance with the outward world, to collect original experiences from things and facts, and to exercise the powers of body and mind. The child indeed recognizes no purpose in it, and knows nothing, in the beginning, of any end which is to be reached when it imitates the play it sees around it, but it expresses its own nature, and that is human nature in its playful activity. (as cited in Von Marenholz-Bulow, 1895, p. 67)

Froebel, like Rousseau, believed in the inherent goodness of the child. Froebel (1887) claimed: 'Therefore, a suppressed or perverted good quality – a good tendency, only repressed, misunderstood, or misguided

– lies originally at the bottom of every shortcoming in man' (p. 121). The natural play of the child, then, allows this goodness to unfold.

Leo Tolstoy

Tolstoy, like Froebel and Pestalozzi, was influenced by Rousseau. He felt that children, and peasant children in particular, should be left untouched so that their goodness can unfold. Tolstoy was very critical of schools:

> School justly presents itself to the child's mind as an establishment where he is taught that which nobody understands; where he is generally compelled to speak not in his native patois, Mundart, but a foreign language; where the teacher for the greater part sees in his pupils, his natural enemies, who, out of their own malice and that of their parents, do not wish to learn that which he has learned; and where the pupils, on their side, look upon their teacher as their enemy. (Weiner, 1967, p. 12)

To provide an alternative, Tolstoy established his own school at Yasnaya Polyana, his estate in Russia, where he taught the peasants according to his own theories. He let the children decide whether they would attend the lessons or not. If they did attend, he had them write stories based on their own experience. Troyat (1980) has given us the flavour of Tolstoy's school:

> At eight in the morning a child rang the bell. Half an hour later, 'through fog, rain, or the slanting rays of the autumn sun,' the black silhouettes of little muzhiks appeared by twos and threes, swinging their empty arms. As in the previous years, they brought no books or notebooks with them – nothing at all, save the desire to learn. The classrooms were painted pink and blue. In one, mineral samples, butterflies, dried plants and physics apparatus lined the shelves. But no books. Why books? The pupils came to the classroom as though it were home; they sat where they liked, on the floor, on the windowledge, on a chair or the corner of a table, they listened or did not listen to what the teacher was saying, drew near when he said something that interested them, left the room when work or play called them elsewhere – but were silenced by their fellow pupils at the slightest sound. Self-imposed discipline. The lessons – if these casual chats between an adult and some children could be called that – went on from eight-thirty to noon and from three to six in the afternoon, and covered

every conceivable subject from grammar to carpentry, by way of religious history, singing, geography, gymnastics, drawing and composition. Those who lived too far away to go home at night slept in the school. In the summer they sat around their teacher outdoors in the grass. Once a week they all went to study plants in the forest. (p. 227)

Bronson Alcott

Bronson Alcott (1799–1888), a friend of both Ralph Waldo Emerson and Henry David Thoreau, devoted much of his life to education. The father of the writer Louisa May Alcott, he struggled throughout his life to support his family, and Emerson frequently came to his aid. In the 1840s Alcott helped found two cooperative communities – Brook Farm and Fruitlands. Fruitlands was a vegetarian community where the members even avoided wearing leather shoes. This community barely lasted a year and could not make it through the winter of 1844.

Alcott believed in the pre-existence of the soul. He thus saw the child as coming into the world not as a *tabula rasa* but as charged with a divine mission. He wrote a manuscript entitled *Observations on the Spiritual Nurture of My Children*, which was based on the idea that each child has a soul that needs to be nurtured and developed. He observed his children and their behaviour and then speculated on the reasons for their behaviour. For example, he wrote: 'Anna is apt to *theorize* both for herself and Louisa; whereas Louisa, intent solely on *practice*, is constantly demolishing Anna's ideal castles and irritating her Spirit with Gothic rudeness. The one builds; the other demolishes; and between the struggle of contrary forces, their tranquillity is disturbed' (as cited in Bedell, p. 83).

While Alcott lived in Philadelphia, he taught at the School of Human Culture, where he tried to nurture the spiritual development of the children. Although this project was short-lived, letters and documents from the school inspired Alcott's friend Elizabeth Peabody to help him start a new school in Boston in 1834. Named the Temple School, this school has its place in the history of holistic education. It was called the Temple School because it was housed in the two rooms at the top of the Masonic Temple, which was directly across from the Boston Commons. Elizabeth Peabody was instrumental in the work of the school. She helped recruit students, taught there, and also recorded many of the 'conversations' that Alcott held with the students there. The school opened in September 1834, and eighteen students were there the first day. The students, between the ages of five and ten, came from some of the most famous families in Boston.

Alcott taught them both reading and writing simultaneously. He had them print the letters first before writing script, 'understanding – as no one had before him – that coordination between hand and eye in writing script was too difficult for young children to master' (Bedell, 1980, p. 94). In writing he wanted the students to express their thoughts and feelings and not just copy something from a book. In discussions Alcott also encouraged the students to stand up and speak out. One student stated, 'I never knew I had a mind till I came to this school'(p. 96). Alcott did not use corporal punishment but instead used abandonment or the threat of abandonment.

By the winter the enrollment had doubled. Elizabeth Peabody, who had first contracted to work just two hours a day, now stayed for the entire school day and began to keep her record of the school. According to Bedell (1980), 'The Record of a School remains today probably the best exploration of Bronson Alcott's theories on education' (p. 102). Published in 1835, the book was part of a larger movement of social change that included women's rights and anti-slavery activities. Bedell suggests that Record of a School became a 'symbol of a whole new era in American thought'(p. 103). Alcott himself had never been happier or felt more fulfilled, writing that he had found 'a *unity* and a *fullness*' (p. 98) in his existence.

The most unusual feature of the school were the conversations that Alcott held with students regarding spiritual matters. Elizabeth Peabody once wrote that 'Education depends on its attitude toward the soul' (p. xvii). Alice Howell (1991) describes how Alcott was able to incorporate this attitude into his teaching:

> That the child is not a *tabula rasa* Alcott proves without a doubt. As we read we rediscover that children are far more capable of philosophical insights and intuitions than we usually think, that indeed they take delight in being taken seriously as individuals whose opinions are worthy of respect ... Alcott's secret, and I believe, his success consisted in his approach to children; he worked from his own innermost center toward the same one he knew existed in each of them. A bond of trust, mutual respect, and affection was established at that level, so that the usual ego-to-ego tussle between teacher and student was avoided. (p. xxxii)

Below is an example of one of his conversations recorded by Elizabeth

Peabody in her book *Record of a School: Exemplifying the General Principles of Spiritual Culture*. The conversation of students took place after Alcott had read passages from the Bible about John the Baptist in the desert. He asked the students: 'What came to mind while I was reading?'

> Josiah: The deserts seemed to me a great space with sand, like that in the hour-glass. The sun was shining on it, and making it sparkle. There were no trees. John was there alone.
> Edward J: I thought the deserts mean woods, with paths here and there.
> Lucy: I thought of a space covered with grass and some wild flowers, and John walking about.
> Charles: I thought of a prairie.
> Alexander: I thought of a few trees scattered over the country, with bees in the trunks.
> George K: I thought of a place without houses, excepting John's; and flowers, trees and bee-hives. (Peabody, 1835, vol. 1, p. 61)

Martin Bickman (2004), who cites this passage, compares this discussion to creative visualization (see Chapter 6). Bickman also comments that Alcott let the conversation go on without acting in the traditional role of the 'central switchboard.' Bickman acknowledges that sometimes Alcott could be manipulative in his teaching but mainly tried to encourage students to find their own imagery and develop their own line of thinking. Bickman cites Dahlstrand (1982) to support his conclusion:

> Alcott's paradigm gave the children a means of experiencing their minds. It served as structure on which they could build ideas. In one sense the paradigm limited them, but in another important way it freed them – it freed them from the tyranny of disorganization. In time they could cast away the paradigm, but the thought processes it helped them develop could stay with them forever ... Almost despite himself, his methods succeeded. (as cited in Bickman, 2004, p. 127)

Another book by Alcott, entitled *Conversations with Children on the Gospels*, was published in 1836, to negative reviews. One writer called Alcott 'either insane or half-witted' (Bedell, 1980, p. 131), while preachers felt that the conversations showed no respect for Christ's divinity. These attacks, combined with debts incurred during an economic recession, led to the closing of the school.

In the Temple School, Alcott developed a *holistic* approach to learning. Martin Bickman (1999) comments: 'The education was what we would now call "holistic," since skills like spelling, grammar, and vocabulary were integrated into larger lessons on ethical and spiritual matters' (p. xxiii). Alcott felt that all teaching and learning should be connected to the spiritual centre, the soul.

A.S. Neill

Perhaps the most famous proponent of humanistic education in the twentieth century was A.S. Neill. Neill founded an alternative school in Germany in 1921 that was later moved to England to become the famous Summerhill school. Like Rousseau, Pestalozzi, and Froebel, Neill disliked moralizing or instilling guilt in children.

At Summerhill, children had the choice of going to class or staying away. Teachers tended to run their classes informally. Croall (1983) writes that Neill 'took virtually no interest in teaching methods, and gave no sort of guidance to his teachers as to what they should be doing' (p. 206). Neill was primarily concerned about the emotional life of the child. Parents often sent problem children to Summerhill, and Neill excelled in responding to their needs. Because they were not forced to learn and because of Neill's caring presence, these children often overcame their difficulties to become healthy individuals. Croall (1983), in his biography of Neill, comments:

Neill's greatest achievement, however, undoubtedly lay in his ability as 'a curer of souls.' A considerable number of adults now leading ordinary unexceptionable lives, owe the fact that they do so to Neill. He himself in later life liked to argue that it was the environment of freedom rather than his individual work with problem children that was responsible for so many startling 'cures.' Many former Summerhill pupils thought otherwise as did several of the adults who worked alongside Neill over the years. To them, it was Neill's humanity and understanding which produced the results. As one former problem child said, looking back over his time at Summerhill: 'I feel almost certain that, had it not been for Neill, I would have ended up in a mental hospital long ago.' (p. 407)

Neill's approach to education stands in contrast to the philosophy of Bertrand Russell, who had established Beacon Hill school in 1927. Once he commented to Russell that if a child were with them, Russell would want the child to tell him about the stars while Neill would prefer to leave to the child with his own thoughts. Croall (1983) concludes that 'while Neill aims to release the emotions, Russell wants to train the mind' (p. 159). Neill believed that if 'the emotions were free, the intellect will look after itself' (as cited in Croall, 1983, p. 219).

Neill was the benign authority at Summerhill. Although students did have a great deal of freedom, Neill drew limits in some areas such as the health and safety of the children and the hiring and firing of teaching staff. For example, he made rules about where the children could climb.

One of the central features of the school was the meeting, where each person had one vote, including Neill. Here his influence was more subtle. Croall (1983) comments:

Nona Simon, who came to Summerhill at the age of 4, and was virtually brought up by the Neills, recalls: 'Most little kids would only vote with the majority, and you'd get just as much hero worship of the older children as of Neill. But he would affect the voting – he was an authority without having to say too much.' Branwen Williams takes a similar view: 'Though he would say that we ran the school, that he had no more say at the meetings than anyone else, I think in practice we still looked to him for a lead – certainly when we were very little. We used to outvote him occasionally, just to prove that his theories were right; but I think we were a little uneasy about it. So there was a subtle kind of guidance.' Cynthia Allen reinforces this idea: 'His very withdrawal from a conflict, his departure to his workshop or desk, made an impact,' she remembers. (p. 181)

Neill, like Rousseau and other romantics, was faced with the dilemma of where and how to intervene in children's lives.

Neill's influence beyond the school was immense. By 1969 his book *Summerhill* was selling at a rate of more than 200,000 copies a year. This book was a bible to many free school educators in the 1960s and 1970s as they attempted to set up their own versions of Summerhill. According to Graubard (1972), the number of free schools reached approximately five hundred by 1972. Graubard claims that these schools did away with

all of the public school apparatus of imposed disciplines and punishments, lock-step gradings and time-period divisions, homework, frequent tests and grades and report cards, rigidly graded curriculum, standardized classrooms, dominated and commanded by one teacher with 25 to 35 students under his or her power. (p. 40)

Unfortunately, these schools did not have Neill as their head. Neill's intuitive genius with children was at the heart of Summerhill's success and could never be replaced in the free schools. Humanistic theory dating back to Rousseau has never been strong and has left zealous educators groping for strategies for dealing with kids.

Ron Miller (2002) has written an extensive analysis of the free school movement. He comments on the long-term legacy of the movement:

> The free school movement, like all human endeavors, contained its own flaws, excesses, and blind spots, but it represented a serious effort to turn society away from the path of sprawling technocracy toward more democratic, holistic, person-centered values. More than opposition to public schooling as such, free school ideology represented conscious deliberate resistance to the spread of technocracy, and this essential element of the 1960's radical education critique continues to resonate in the literature of alternative, progressive and holistic education. (p. 179)

Open Education Movement

Most of the free schools sprang up outside the public school system. However, many public school educators sought their own form of humanistic education. Public school systems have implemented open education and various forms of affective education. Charles Silberman's book *Crisis in the Classroom* (1970) put open education into the limelight in the United States, while in Ontario the *Hall-Dennis Report* (1968) did the same. Open education was an attempt to implement a more child-centred approach in schools through a variety of techniques such as interest centres, classrooms without walls, team teaching, individualized instruction, and more choices for learners. Affective education employed various strategies such as values clarification, simulation games, and role-playing to enhance the emotional development of the student.

Ravitch (1983) claims the open education movement failed:

> The open education movement ... did not survive as a movement because, lacking a definition, it became identified with ideas and practices of its extremely child-centered advocates, those who zealously opposed what-

ever was traditional in the structure, content, or methods of the classroom. Their ideological tenets stressed the freedom of the child, the passivity of the teacher, equality between teacher and child, the virtues of play and unstructured activity, and distrust of extrinsic motivation. Open classroom teachers who expected their methods to work as the ideology said it would were in for a rude awakening. Nothing prepared them for criticism from parents and other teachers about the noisiness of their classrooms and the neglect of 'basics.' They were taken aback when children demanded that teachers take a more active role or asked to learn from a textbook; they did not know how to deal with discipline problems because they were not supposed to have any. (pp. 254–5)

While open education may have failed in bringing about many of the changes that it intended, I believe that this judgment is too harsh and too limited. Open education and affective education did instil a basic concern for treating students with more respect. Now teachers more fully recognize the importance of student self-concept as vital to learning and development. In a more legalistic sense, there is a much stronger recognition of the limits of the teacher's arbitrary authority in dealing with students.

Social Change Education

Social change educators believe that society needs change, often of a radical nature, and that schools have an important role to play in bringing it about. It is possible to view Plato's *Republic* as one of the first social change documents that outlined the importance of education in creating a new society. Karl Marx believed that education had been used by the capitalists to maintain their economic interests. Marxists have claimed that the hidden curriculum of the school reinforces passivity so that workers will accept their role on the assembly line. Textbooks avoid controversial issues and help in the development of the 'good citizen' who does what he or she is told. However, Marx also saw the potential of education in bringing about fundamental change by making people more conscious of their exploitation.

In the twentieth century Francisco Ferrer, George Counts, and Myles Horton have argued for social change or reconstruction.

Francisco Ferrer

In 1901 Francisco Ferrer began the Escuela Moderna for the workers' children of Barcelona, Spain. Ferrer developed an approach called 'rational education,' in which the teachers develop the children's critical faculties through inquiry and scientific investigation. Ferrer stated:

> The distinction between justice and injustice is perhaps the first moral distinction which a child can and does grasp and it would be ridiculous to pretend it lies outside the proper sphere of education. Our intrinsic plea that it is not fair to prejudice the mind of a child on subjects he cannot fully understand is nothing but a fallacy of bourgeois self defence. (as cited in Archer, 1911, p. 48)

Unlike Rousseau or Tolstoy, Ferrer was not content to leave children to their own devices. Instead, he felt that they should be immersed in social issues so that they can develop a critical awareness of social forces. Ferrer suggested that critical literature can help raise the child's consciousness:

> It penetrates to their intelligence and implants in them a rooted conviction of the possibility of a new order of things in which peace and happiness shall reign supreme, very unlike our present condition of social injustice, strife and unhappiness. (as cited in Archer, 1911, p. 40)

Ferrer particularly liked Jean Grave's *The Adventures of Nono*, which builds revolutionary ideas into a fantasy tale. In this story a ten-year-old boy goes through a series of adventures in places such as 'Autonomy' and 'Solidarity' and meets people such as 'The Capitalist' and 'The Workers.' When Nono receives a gift from his parents, Grave draws the following point: 'not an expensive one, of course, for the parents of Nono were working people, and the rich people squander money on frivolities to such a degree that scarcely anything is left over for the working people to buy their children what they require' (Archer, 1911, p. 40).

Ferrer encouraged parents to participate in his school. He also edited a magazine that focused on syndicalism as well as articles on radical education. Ferrer's work had a strong impact on radical schools in France and Italy and eventually the Modern School in New York.

The Modern School

Ferrer was executed in 1910 for his alleged involvement in an assassination attempt on Spain's royal couple, providing the impetus for the foundation of the Ferrer Association in New York, which was modelled on the ideals of Ferrer and Tolstoy. The Association founded the Ferrer Center, the Modern School, and a journal, *The Modern School*. The Association consisted of workers, socialists, anarchists, and libertarians. Some of the more militant leaders included Emma Goldman and Alexander Berman. The goals of the Association were:

1. To create an education center for radical thought that would provide evening classes and a radical reading room consisting of radical literature not available elsewhere in the community.
2. To continue the protests of Ferrer's execution.
3. To found a day school for children along the lines of the Modern School of Spain.
4. To aid all movements for liberation. (Kelly, 1913, p. 57)

The school opened in 1911 and the founders believed that libertarian and socialist principles could be combined. The school was based on the belief that children 'raised in freedom would refuse oppressive working conditions and become political revolutionaries' (Trager, 1986, p. 401). The Modern School was housed in the same building as the Association and contained portraits of Ferrer, Tolstoy, Whitman, Ibsen, and William Morris. The radical magazine *Mother Earth* was published in its offices. According to Trager (1986), initially the pedagogy at the Modern School was based on Tolstoy's writings:

The classroom methodology was libertarian in the Tolystoyean sense. Children arrived at the school when they wished and worked and played at their own pace on the subjects that interested them. The curriculum was often defined by the children themselves. A typical day at the Modern School was described by Will Durant, the teacher at the school in the winter of 1912–1913. According to Durant, the children arrived at different times. When he arrived the children ran to tackle him and continued their friskiness for the next half hour. Then some children studied and worked while others continued rough-housing. Those that were ready for work went into the quiet room where they did lessons in reading and mathematics or did encyclopedia work. The eight older children were given lessons every day while the younger children received their individual instruction approximately every other day. When the weather permitted, the children would have a picnic lunch in the park and spend the afternoon outside playing and telling stories. (as cited in Trager, 1986, p. 402)

Trager points out that there were inevitable conflicts between the political radicals and the libertarians about what philosophy the school should take. Although Ferrer remained the guiding image of the school, the day-to-day life in the school was more Tolstoyean. However, the Ferrer Center, which attracted political radicals, influenced the children and the school in a more informal way. Thus, a synthesis of the revolutionary and libertarian strands was effected. One student said, 'As much as the Day School meant to me, the center meant more ... That's where things were happening! I got to know people from all parts of the world and all parts of the radical spectrum' (p. 404).

Members of the Ferrer Association taught at the school, and children attended adult classes which were held at the centre. This was also a period of intense political activity with strikes and demonstrations occuring frequently in New York. This overall climate also had an impact on the school.

Some parents expressed concern about the relaxed curriculum and atmosphere of the school, and as a result more academic subjects were added with a stress on history. Classroom activity became less individualistic and more group oriented. Students contributed to a children's magazine and the decoration of the classroom. Eventually the school moved to Stelton, New Jersey, where, under the leadership of Alex and Elizabeth Ferm, the school again adopted a more Tolstoyean stance. In general, it was during the New York years that the real synthesis of romantic and political education took place.

George S. Counts

George Counts was influenced by John Dewey's social activism. Counts was most famous for his book *Dare the Schools Build a New Social Order?* which was published in 1932. Horrified by the Depression and unemployment, Counts visited Russia in 1930 and felt the United States should deal more constructively with the problems it faced. Counts was critical of progressive education, which he felt attempted to avoid controversy under the guise of value-neutrality. He wrote:

If Progressive Education is to be genuinely progressive, it must emancipate itself from the influence of this class, face squarely and courageously every social issue, come to grips with life in all of its stark reality, establish an organic relation with the community, develop a realistic and comprehensive theory of welfare, fashion a compelling and challenging vision of human destiny, and become less frightened than it is today at the bogies of imposition and indoctrination. (1932, pp. 9–10)

Critics said that Counts was a communist sympathizer, and his call for fundamental change was not accepted by mainstream educators. However, his plea for teachers to become involved in social change continues to prod the consciences of educators.

Myles Horton

Perhaps no person represents the holistic approach to social change education more than Myles Horton. Horton was associated with the Highlander Folk School in Monteagle, Tennessee, from its founding in 1932 until his death in 1990. This school was involved in a number of social change initiatives including the civil rights movement. In his autobiography, *The Long Haul* (1998), Horton describes the Citizenship School, which was connected to Highlander. It helped educate blacks so that they could vote. Horton describes the first Citizenship School and its teacher Bernice Robinson:

> Bernice began the first class in the back room of the cooperative store by saying. 'I am not a teacher, we are here to learn together. You're going to teach me as much I'm going to teach you.' She had no textbooks or teacher's manuals. Her only materials were the UN Declaration of Human Rights, the state constitution ...
>
> Bernice and the students developed the curriculum day by day. They learned to write letters, order catalogs and fill out money orders. They made up stories about the vegetables they grew and the tools they used.
>
> 'They tell me a story,' Mrs. Robinson told us, 'a story which I write down , then they learn to read the story, It's their story in their words, and they are interested because it's theirs.' She gave priority to their immediate interests so they could experience the usefulness and joy of learning. (p. 103)

These Citizenship schools started to spread throughout the southern United States and helped many blacks participate in the voting process. The educational approach to literacy is similar to Sylvia Ashton-Warner's approach to teaching the Maori children in New Zealand, which is described in Chapter 8.

Horton (1998) articulates his view of holistic education:

I have a holistic view of the educative process. The universe is one: nature and mind and spirit and the heavens and time and the future all are part of the big ball of life. Instead of thinking that you put pieces together that will add up to a whole, I think you have to start with the premise that they're already together and you try to keep from destroying life by segmenting it, overorganizing it and dehumanizing it. You try to keep things together. The educative process must be organic, and not an assortment of unrelated methods or ideas. (p. 130)

The Long Haul is an inspiring document, and it is clear Horton embodied an approach to social change that was rooted in a holistic perspective.

Conclusion

The definitive work on the history of holistic education is Ron Miller's *What Are Schools For? Holistic Education in American Culture* (1997), and I strongly recommend the reader consult that work. Miller (2002) has also written an important book on the free school movement. Other examples of holistic education include the work of Ruldolf Steiner and Maria Montessori, who will be discussed later in this book since their work is still very much part of the contemporary educational scene.

References

Archer, W. (1911). *The life, trial, and death of Francisco Ferrer*. London: Chapman & Hall.

Bayles, E.E., & Hood, B.L. (1966). *Growth of American educational thought and practice*. New York: Harper & Row.

Bedell, M. (1980). *The Alcotts: Biography of a family*. New York: Crown.

Bickman, M. (Ed.). (1999). *Uncommon learning: Henry David Thoreau on education*. Boston: Houghton Mifflin Co.

Bickman, M. (2004). *Minding American education: Reclaiming the tradition of active learning*. New York: Teachers College Press

Counts, G. (1932). *Dare the schools build a new social order?* New York: Day.

Croall, J. (1983). *Neill of Summerhill: The permanent rebel*. London: Routledge and Kegan Paul.

Dahlstrand, F.C. (1982). *Amos Bronson Alcott: An intellectual biography*. East Brunswick, NJ: Associated University Presses.

Damrosch, L. (2005). Jean Jacques Rousseau: Restless giant. New York: Houghton Mifflin.

de Guimps, R. (1889). *Pestalozzi: His aim and work.* Syracuse, NY: C.W. Bardeen.

Froebel, F. (1887). *The education of man.* New York: Appleton-Century Crofts.

Graubard, A. (1972). *Free the children: Radical reform and the free school movement.* New York: Pantheon.

Hadot, P. (2002). *What is ancient philosophy?* Cambridge, MA: Belknap Press.

Horton, M. (1998). *The long haul: An autobiography.* New York: Teachers College Press.

Howell, A.O. (1991). Introduction. In A.B. Alcott, *How like an angel came I down* (pp. xvii–xliv). Hudson, NY: Lindisfarne Press.

Kelly. (1913). A short history of the Francisco Ferrer Association, *The Modern School* (Autumn).

McEvilley, T. (2002). *The shape of ancient thought: Comparative studies in Greek and Indian philosophies.* New York: Allworth Press.

Miller, R. (1997). *What are schools for? Holistic education in American culture.* (2nd ed.). Brandon, VT: Holistic Education Press.

Miller, R. (2002) *Free schools, free people: Education and democracy after the 1960s.* Albany: State University of New York Press.

Ontario Department of Education. (1968). *Living and learning: The Hall-Dennis report* . Toronto: Ontario Department of Education.

Ozman, H.A., & Craver, S.M. (1981). *Philosophical foundations of education.* Columbus, OH: Charles E. Merrill.

Peabody, E. (1835). *Record of a school: Exemplifying the general principles of spiritual culture.* Boston: James Munroe.

Ravitch, D. (1983). *The troubled crusade: American education 1945–1980.* New York: Basic.

Rousseau, J.J. (1955). *Émile.* New York: Everyman's Library.

Silberman, C. (1970). *Crisis in the classroom.* New York: Random House.

Trager, F. (1986). Politics and culture in anarchist education: The Modern School of New York and Stelton 1911–1915. *Curriculum Inquiry, 16*(4), 391–416.

Troyat, H. (1980). *Tolstoy.* New York: Crown Publishers, Harmony.

Von Marenholz-Bulow, B. (1895). *Reminiscences of Friedrich Froebel.* Boston: Lee & Sheppard.

Weiner, L. (Trans.). (1967). *Tolstoy on education.* Chicago: University of Chicago Press.

PART TWO

Holistic Curriculum: Practice

CHAPTER SIX

Intuitive Connections

At the beginning of the book I offered the following definition of holistic education:

> The focus of holistic education is on relationships: the relationship between linear thinking and intuition, the relationship between mind and body, the relationships among various domains of knowledge, the relationship between the individual and community, the relationship to the earth, and our relationship to our souls. In the holistic curriculum the student examines these relationships so that he or she gains both an awareness of them and the skills necessary to transform the relationships where it is appropriate.

The second part of this book explores these connections and examines teaching strategies associated with them. The following is an outline of the topics of Part Two:

1. *Linear thinking and intuition:* The holistic curriculum attempts to restore a balance between linear thinking and intuition. In Chapter 6 I discuss the nature of intuition, how we can attempt to link it with linear forms of cognition, and how we can use various techniques such as metaphor and visualization to enhance its role in the classroom. This chapter also explores critical thinking and approaches that attempt to synthesize various forms of thinking, such as Gardner's multiple intelligences.
2. *Mind and body:* As discussed in Chapter 7, the holistic curriculum explores the relationship between mind and body so the student can sense the connection between the two. The relationship can be explored through movement, drama, dance, and yoga.

3. *Domains of knowledge:* Chapter 8 looks at the many different ways we can connect academic disciplines and school subjects. For example, Waldorf education connects subjects through the arts. The relationship between self and subject matter is also examined as well as the connection between subject matter and community. I also discuss holistic approaches to thinking that can link subjects.

4. *Self and community:* As discussed in chapter 9, the holistic curriculum sees the student in relation to his or her community. Community refers to the classroom community, the school community, the community of one's town or city, and the global community. The student develops interpersonal skills, community service skills, and social action skills.

5. *Relationship with the Earth:* One of the most important connections is our relationship with the Earth and related organic processes. Many ecologists argue that we have lost this connection. Chapter 10 looks at how by being in nature and also studying the writings of those who have not lost their 'original relation to the universe' we can gradually begin to see ourselves as part of the web of life.

6. *Self and soul:* Ultimately the holistic curriculum lets us realize our true nature. In Chapter 11, a curriculum for the inner life is presented. Science can also nurture the inner life through the universe story. Chapter 11 examines the role of contemplation in the classroom.

Logic and Intuition

The holistic curriculum connects linear thinking and intuition. There has been a great deal of focus on right and left brain learning and, although this research is interesting, I do not believe it should be the focus for connecting conceptual thought and intuition. First, the right brain/ left brain theme has been overworked and the educational connections to the brain research are often not well grounded. Second, there is the danger of getting caught in physiological reductionism by attempting to link all forms of knowing to the brain. From a holistic perspective, it is possible to see the whole human body, including the smallest cell, as learning, growing, and developing.

What Is Intuition?

Intuition is a direct knowing. In contrast, linear cognition involves a

sequential, observable process. Noddings and Shore (1984) characterize intuition as 'seeing without glasses, hearing without filters, touching with ungloved hand. The immediate character of intuition does not
imply accuracy, rightness, or moral goodness. It does imply commitment and clarity' (p. 57). In the intuitive mode there is no mediator.
Noddings and Shore derive their view of intuition from Kant and Schopenhauer. From Kant comes the view of intuition as direct knowing
and from Schopenhauer the idea that intuition is linked to the will. For
Noddings and Shore, the will is the 'dynamic center of self, the heart of
being' (p. 59); in other words, it is similar to what I have referred to as
the self or centre. The will directs intuition and 'subordinates analytic
and algorithmic activity to its needs, quieting the continual humming
of the internal logic machine' (p. 59).

Levels of Intuition

Frances Vaughan (1979) has described four levels of intuition: physical, emotional, mental, and spiritual. The *physical* level of intuition is
characterized by a strong bodily response – for example, the awareness
that people in the jungle can have when they sense physical danger.
Intuition, however, differs from instinct in that the person is fully conscious, while instinct is more unconscious. Intuitions at this level are
also related to the body–mind connection. For example, the body will
give the first clues that a person is experiencing stress. Muscle tension,
or muscle spasms, can indicate that we need to examine the sources
of stress in our life. Vaughan argues that we should learn to trust the
responses of our body. A study by Charles Tart (1975) supports this
conclusion. In this experiment a subject in a soundproof chamber was
asked to tap a telegraph key when he felt he had received a 'subliminal
stimulus.' This subject was not given a direct stimulus; but in another
soundproof room, a person was receiving a low-level electric shock.
This second person tried to send a telepathic message to the first person
each time he received a shock so that he would strike the telegraph key.
Interestingly, the key taps were unrelated to the mental messages but
bodily responses were related to the mental messages. Brain wave and
heart rate measurements indicated that the first person was responding
to the messages, although he was not conscious of it.

At the *emotional* level the person experiences intuition through feelings. For example, we can pick up 'vibrations' from people we meet.
Sometimes these feelings can be quite intense; other times they are more

subtle. Vaughan claims that what we refer to as woman's intuition is the emotional level, although this is largely a culturally imposed view of intuition. An example of emotional intuition is given by Vaughan (1979):

> When I was in graduate school a friend of mine had told me how much he wanted to get to know one of our professors whom he greatly admired. One night he dreamed that he was talking to him, but the professor did not say much, and refused to take off his overcoat. As my friend reflected on what the dream was telling him, he realized that he had felt intuitively that this man had wanted to keep his distance ever since they met. Repeated attempts to get better acquainted were of no avail. He later regretted the time and effort expended, for he had 'known' all along that it would be fruitless. (p. 71)

Sometimes emotional intuition can be the source of artistic expression, even though it is difficult to describe the connection between the original intuition and its final expression. Elizabeth Herron (as cited in Vaughan, 1979), a contemporary poet, describes the difficulties of expressing her intuitive insights:

> I was depressed. The world had gone flat and colorless. I had withdrawn. I was a tiny kernel inside my body, adrift amid necessities and obligations, oppressed by my separateness, cut off from the wellsprings of my soul. I walked up to the pond, took off my clothes and plunged into the water a sudden shock, cold against my skin. Floating to the surface, I heard a bird call across the meadow. Suddenly, I was at the stillpoint. The bird's call was my voice. We were separate and yet one. I was out there and in here ... All things converged in me and radiated from me. 'The center of the circle is everywhere, the circumference nowhere.' I recognized this, knowing it had always been so, though I had been cut off from my experience of it. My head filled with poetic images. The dimension of the infinite was everywhere.
>
>   This was a repetition of similar experiences. It is a paradoxical awareness. In these moments I know. But my knowing is not enough. I must struggle to comprehend what I know. My intuitive knowledge must be expressed in order to be communicated. I cannot share my experience merely by telling you about it. As a poet, I seek words for my experience, but words alone are not enough. There are realities nuances of feeling and meaning, for which words are inadequate. (p. 72)

At the *mental* level intuition is often expressed through images. Here we may have flashes of insight that can lead to scientific inquiry. David Bohm (1984) describes a high level of mental intuition as insight. For Bohm insight is 'an act of perception permeated with intense energy and passion, that brings about great clarity ... This perception includes new forms of imagination and new orders of reason' (p. 15). Bohm states, 'Those who knew Einstein will agree that his work was permeated with great passion' (p. 54). Einstein's passionate insight led him to move beyond the existing Newtonian paradigm to develop the theory of relativity.

One of the vehicles for intuitive insight is the mental image. Einstein said, 'The words or the language, as they are written or spoken, do not seem to play any role in my mechanism of thought. The physical entities which seem to serve as elements in thought are certain signs and more or less clear images which can be "voluntarily" reproduced and combined' (cited in Vaughan, 1979, p. 72). Einstein believed that objective reality can only be truly grasped by intuition, not by empiricism or logic. Muller-Markus (1976) says, 'An idea like Planck's quantum of action was not logically entailed by experiment, nor could it be derived from previous theories. Planck conceived it out of his own self' (p. 154).

Vaughan claims that the 'Aha' experience of insight is another example of mental intuition. Sometimes the 'Aha' experience can involve an insight into one's own behaviour, or, alternatively, it can involve a creative solution to a problem. Melvin Calvin (1976), a Nobel laureate in chemistry, gives the following example of mental intuition:

> One day I was waiting in my car while my wife was on an errand. I had had for some months some basic information from the laboratory which was incompatible with everything which, up until then, I knew about the photosynthetic process. I was waiting, sitting at the wheel, most likely parked in the red zone, when the recognition of the missing compound occurred. It occurred just like that quite suddenly and suddenly, also, in a matter of seconds, the cyclic character of the path of carbon became apparent to me, not in the detail which ultimately was elucidated, but the original recognition of phosphoglyceric acid, and how it got there, and how the acceptor might be regenerated, all occurred in a matter of 30 seconds. (p. 2)

The highest level of intuition is the *spiritual*. Here intuition is independent from feeling, thoughts, and sensations. Vaughan (1979) comments: 'Paradoxically, the cues on which intuition depends on the other levels are regarded as interference at this level' (p. 77). James Bugental (1976) has said, 'Man knows God in his deepest intuitions about his own nature' (p. 296). At the spiritual level intuition moves beyond dualism to experience unity directly. The following statement by Teilhard de Chardin (1965) is an example of spiritual intuition:

> The farther and more deeply we penetrate into matter, by means of increasingly powerful methods, the more we are confounded by the interdependence of its parts. Each element of the cosmos is positively woven from all the others ... It is impossible to cut into this network, to isolate a portion without it becoming frayed and unraveled at all its edges. All around us, as far as the eye can see, the universe holds together, and only one way of considering it is really possible, that is, to take it as a whole, in one piece. (pp. 43–4)

Meditation is a technique designed to quiet the mind so that spiritual intuition can arise. One type of meditation is visualization, which is discussed later in this chapter.

Intuition and Education

Why should we focus on intuition in education and seek to balance analytic thought with intuitive insight? First, there is some evidence that intuition is integral to creativity. Wallas (1926) describes four basic elements in the creative process. The first step is *preparation*, in which the individual gathers information relevant to the problem or project. At the second stage, *incubation*, the individual relaxes and does not make an effort to work consciously on the problem. Instead, it is suggested that the images realign themselves in the individual as he or she consciously attends to something else. In the *illumination* state the solution will occur, often spontaneously and unexpectedly, as in case of the chemist Melvin Calvin, mentioned above. The second and third stages, then, are the intuitive, while the first and fourth stages are more analytical. The fourth stage is *verification*, or *revision*, where the individual puts the idea into use and consciously works with the idea in a more detailed manner.

The Wallas model, and other models of creative thinking, are useful to the educator in balancing analysis and insight in classroom pedagogy. Visualization, meditation, and various aesthetic experiences can be used to enhance incubation and illumination, while logical problem-solving models can be used to facilitate preparation and verification (Beyer, 1991). Effective thinking, then, involves both intuition and analysis.

Einstein and Mozart are examples of individuals who were able to effectively relate both analysis and insight at the highest level. If our thinking is dominated by one mode, it is much less effective. If the emphasis is on linear, analytic thinking, we can become plodding in our approach and lose spontaneity in dealing with problems. If we stress the intuitive, then we can lose our ground. Our ideas can become irrelevant if we make no attempt to verify them. Generally schools have not emphasized the teaching of thinking skills (Ross & Maynes, 1982, p. 2), and when they have, it has usually been linear problem solving rather than a more holistic approach.

Another reason for an intuitive pedagogy is outlined in the research of Jerome Singer (1976), which suggests that the risks of an undeveloped imagination include 'delinquency, violence, overeating and the use of dangerous drugs' (p. 32). According to Singer's research, this tendency appears early in children who are impulsive, who are excessively dependent, and who lack a developed inner life. Children who can use their imagination tend to be more relaxed and independent in their behaviour. This trend continues into adolescence. Another study revealed that in a child guidance clinic, imaginative children were less likely to be violent. Like the other children in the clinic, they were emotionally troubled but they exhibited their difficulties in less aggressive ways than their unimaginative peers. These studies indicate that those individuals with an underdeveloped inner life seem to be more vulnerable to external stimuli. Thus, a developed inner life connected to intuition and imagination can be a source of autonomy.

Andrew Weil (1972) argues that intuitive consciousness, or what he calls non-linear consciousness, is 'an innate, normal drive, analogous to hunger or the sexual drive' (p. 19). According to Weil, if there is no chance to express our non-linear consciousness, we can resort to drug and alcohol abuse. He suggests that the need to explore non-linear consciousness begins early in life: young children often like to 'whirl themselves into vertiginous stupors' (p. 19). Children also hyperventilate and have other children spin them around until they almost faint. They may even choke each other to lose consciousness. As children sense that the culture does not accept their interest in non-linear consciousness, they may push the interest underground. Exploring the inner life becomes a private experience that is shared only with their most intimate friends.

Weil (1972) observed this developmental trend in working with individuals who had drug problems. He summarizes this trend by referring to his own life:

> I feel confident about this developmental scheme for two reasons. First, I have seen it clearly in the histories of many hundreds of drug users I have interviewed and known. Second, I have experienced it myself. I was an avid whirler and could spend hours collapsed on the ground with the world spinning around this despite the obvious unpleasant side effects of nausea, dizziness, and sheer exhaustion (the only aspects of the experience visible to grownups). From my point of view these effects were incidental to a state of consciousness that was extraordinarily fascinating – more interesting than any other state except the one I entered at the verge of sleep. I soon found out that my spinning made grownups upset; I learned to do it with other neighborhood children in out-of-the-way locations, and I kept it up until I was nine or ten. At about the age of four, like most members of my generation, I had my tonsils out, and the experience of ether anesthesia (administered by the old-fashioned open-drop method) remains one of my strongest memories of early life. It was frightening, intensely interesting, and intimately bound up with my thoughts about death. Some years later I discovered that a particular brand of cleaning fluid in the basement of my house gave me a similar experience, and I sniffed it many times, often in the company of others my age. I could not have explained what I was doing to anyone; the experience was interesting rather than pleasant, and I knew it was important to me to explore its territory. (pp. 24–5)

Intuition in the Classroom

We can build intuition into our pedagogy in several ways. In this section I discuss two methods: visualization and metaphor.

Visualization

Visualization uses a set of images in either a directed or undirected manner and is sometimes referred to as guided imagery. Using the mind's eye, the person follows a particular set of images; for example, the individual can imagine herself climbing a mountain. The mountain climb is often symbolic of psychological and spiritual growth. In the undirected visualization the person may start with a few general guidelines and wait for images to appear. Undirected visualization can be used in problem solving.

Research indicates the positive effects of visualization. For example, Michael Murphy (1992) claims that these 'studies have shown that imagery practice can facilitate relief from various afflictions, among them depression, anxiety, insomnia, obesity, sexual problems, chronic pain, phobias, psychosomatic illnesses, cancer, and other diseases' (p. 372). The Simontons (1978) conducted research which indicates that visualization has helped cancer patients. Their studies show that visualization increases the quality of life, lengthens life expectancy, and in a small percentage of cases may have contributed to remission of the disease (Simonton & Matthews-Simonton, 1978). Other studies (Samuels & Samuels, 1975) indicate that visualization is helpful in overcoming the effects of stress. Systematic desensitization is a technique that employs visualization to help people overcome phobias. The person imagines herself in a stressful situation (e.g., the dentist's office) but deals with the stress in a more relaxed manner.

Visualization has been used a great deal in sports. Studies have indicated that it is helpful in improving performance. Richardson (1969) has shown the effects of visualization on the free throws of basketball players. One group in the study practised free throws everyday for twenty days. A second group made free throws only on the first and twentieth days with no practice in between. The third group made free throws on the first and twentieth days but spent twenty minutes each day visualizing sinking baskets. The first group, the one that actually practised, improved 24 per cent between the first and last days. The second group, the one that did not practise, did not improve at all. However, the third group, the one that did the visual practice, improved 23 per cent between the first and last days. Richardson found that it was important for the visualizer to control the image. For example, one subject who had trouble visualizing bouncing the ball did not improve as much as the others did.

As noted earlier, undirected imagery can be helpful in the creative process. In Wallas's model the illumination phase often occurs through imagery. Ainsworth-Land (1982) has described the relationship between imagery and creativity in a developmental manner and describes first-order imaging as sense-related and arising from physical need. The creative product at this level is usually realistic and concrete. Second-order imaging is more predictable and often involves improvement of an existing idea or artistic product. Analysis and evaluation are often second-order imaging processes. The goal is also clear and may involve curing cancer, stopping smoking, or overcoming the effects of stress. Synthesis is usually found in third-order creativity and imagery. Here the product not only is a revision or modification, as in second-order creativity, but involves something novel. Thus, there is a breakthrough to a new level of thinking. The fourth and final level of creativity and imaging involves the 'ultimate form of relatedness' (p. 17). Ainsworth-Land states: 'One's whole being comes into play with the conscious and unconscious minds, reason and intuition, inner and outer, subsumed into a kind of meta-consciousness' (p. 17). The poet William Blake called this order 'four-fold vision' in which a person sometimes feels that he is being guided by a force greater than himself. The four levels of imagery and creativity are shown in Figure 6.1.

Visualization in the Classroom

Visualization can be used to facilitate relaxation, to help motivate student interest in the subject matter, and to facilitate creative writing. Below I give one example in each of these areas.

In doing visualization in the classroom, you should let the students know that they are in control of their own images. There is no 'right' image for the visualization, since the images will differ for each person. If students find it hard to visualize, they should just relax and listen to the visualization. If an image appears that makes the students frightened or tense, they can just open their eyes.

RELAXATION

Lie down on the ground and close your eyes. Focus for a few seconds on your breath, feeling relaxed with each exhalation. We then begin to relax each part of the body and we start this process by tensing the muscles in the body and then relaxing them. Begin first with the feet: tense the muscles in the feet, hold the tension for a few seconds, and then let go. Now repeat this with the ankles and calf muscles: tighten, hold, and let go. Feel the body becoming relaxed as you do this. Now concentrate on the thigh muscles: tighten, hold, and let go. Move to the buttocks: tighten, hold, and let go. Focus now on the abdomen: tighten,

Figure 6.1 Developmental Integration of Creativity and Imaging

Imaging		Creativity	
Orders	Self-involvement	Product	Processes
1st order: ⟶ Spontaneous, sense-based, concrete, direct representation, realistic	Non-awareness of 'self,' creating out of seed, survival motivation, 'self-creating'	Realistic, concrete representation, discovery learning, memory building, invention	Perceiving, exploring, spontaneous acting
2nd order: ⟶ Comfortable, predictable, aware of ability to manipulate and control, analogical, comparative	Belonging, self-extension, goal directing, ego building and verifying, self-consciousness	Improvements and modifications, impressions, strengthening and enhancing, analogical	Categorizing, comparing, analysing, evaluating
3rd order: ⟶ Abstract, symbolic, super-imposing, metaphorical, controlled, and spontaneous	Sharing differences, 'selves' realization and reintegration, giving up rigid control, opening to 'flow'	Innovation, integrated synthesis of old and new abstractions, symbols	Abstracting, synthesizing, metaphorical thinking, intuiting
4th order: ⟶ Renunciation of control, chaotic, psychedelic, illuminating receptivity to unconscious material	Self as part of larger reality, 'meta-consciousness,' disintegration of barriers: conscious-unconscious	Invention of new order, new paradigm, philosophical shifts, new pattern formation, 'inspired' creations	Disintegrating, surrendering, accepting, opening, building new perceptual order

hold, and let go. Now move to the chest muscles: tighten, hold, and let go. Focus on the shoulders: tighten, hold, and let go. Feel the body relax. Tighten the arms now, hold, and let go. Move to the neck: tighten, hold, and let go. Now tighten the facial muscles, hold, and let go. Finally, tighten the whole body, hold, and let go.

Now visualize yourself on an elevator that is descending. As the elevator goes down, feel yourself becoming calm and relaxed. I will count down from five to one and as I count down see yourself in the elevator, descending and relaxing. Five ... Four ... Three ... Two ... One. Now you emerge from the elevator and you walk into an open field. It is warm and sunny. You walk for a while and then decide to lie down in the soft, fresh grass.

As you lie there, visualize around your heart a pure white light. This light is full of warmth and energy. Now see the light expand gradually throughout your body and as it expands you feel relaxed and ener- gized ... Know that anytime you can connect with this light and energy. Open your eyes now, feeling refreshed and energized.

MOTIVATION / SUBJECT MATTER

Beverly-Colleene Gaylean (1983) wrote a book that is filled with visu- alization activities for different subjects. She claims that after visualiza- tion activities students

1. are more attentive
2. enjoy the learning experience more
3. do more original and creative work
4. get along better with their classmates
5. feel more confident
6. are more relaxed
7. do better on tests (p. 25)

One example of using visualization in science is to have students imagine magnetic fields around a transformer. The students can see themselves as electrons in the wire of the coil and experience the move- ment generated by the rapidly changing force field. Then the students can visualize themselves as electrons moving faster and faster as the two fields surrounding the coils interact and come closer.

Another example of a visualization in science is to have students imagine themselves as white blood cells moving through the circula- tory system in the human body. First, they visualize the blood being recirculated through the heart. The students can also imagine the white cells and their role in the immune system in fighting disease.

It is also possible to have students use imagery in languages and social studies. In social studies the students could imagine them- selves as a historical figure facing a particular choice and visualizing the thoughts and emotions that accompanied the decision. The stu- dents could also visualize themselves as Loyalists coming to Canada and imagining their thoughts and feelings as they begin life in a new country.

Other subjects where visualization has been used successfully include mathematics (Arcavi, 2003; Wheatley, 1998), geography (Chatterjea, 1999) and reading instruction (Eisenwine, Fowler & McKenzie, 2000).

CREATIVE WRITING

One of the best uses of visualization in the classroom is as a source of ideas for creative writing. Williams (1983) provides an example:

> Select a piece of music that evokes strong images for you. Play it for the class (after a relaxation exercise and suitable introduction) and ask them to let the music suggest images, moods, feelings, and sensations to them. Tell them to be receptive to whatever comes to them as the music plays. Afterward, ask them to talk or write about the experience in either prose or poetry. You can start with prose and select the strongest images to form the basis for poetry; or one or two strong images may serve as the basis for a longer prose piece. This fantasy can also be used as a stimulus for an art project. If you use it for both visual and verbal expression, you might devote some class time to discussing how the experiences differed (some students will prefer writing, others painting; it's a matter of personal style). (p. 133)

Visualization improves with practice. Generally, the more students use it the more varied their ideas and the more comfortable they feel with the process. A good source of visualization exercises for elementary school children is *Spinning Inward* by Maureen Murdock (1982). Below is one that can be used for creative writing:

> Close your eyes and focus your attention on your breath. Gently breathe in ... and ... out. As you breathe quietly and calmly, your body becomes more and more relaxed. Now imagine that you are sitting outside in the grass and it's a beautiful warm sunny day. You enjoy looking at all of the new spring flowers. You enjoy their colors and smells. All of a sudden you see a little person in front of you, climbing up the stem of a lovely white daisy. This person is no bigger than your middle finger and turns to you and motions to you to follow. You realize that you, yourself, have become little and you hurry to follow your new friend. You now have three minutes of clocktime equal to all of the time you need to have an adventure

with this flower fairy. (after three minutes) Now it is time to say goodbye to your friend and to come back here filled with the memories of your adventure. I will count to 10. Please join me at the count of 6 and open your eyes feeling alert and refreshed at the count of 10. (p. 106)

Another excellent resource is *Emotional Healing and Self-Esteem* by Mark Pearson (1998). Pearson develops the concept of inner life skills, which include visualization, meditation, and relaxation. Pearson has found that these skills lead to the following outcomes:

- increased ability to concentrate
- greater sense of well being
- emotional stability
- improved interpersonal relations
- increased creativity

Pearson's book is filled with a variety of activities for children and adolescents. Other visualization exercises can be found in my books *Education and the Soul* (2000) and *The Holistic Teacher* (1993).

Ellen Handle Spitz (2006) writes more generally about children's imagination. She argues that the emphasis on accountability has meant that education has continued to ignore the inner life of children. She writes:

Against the grain of current educational fetishes for testing children's cognitive abilities, measuring their factual knowledge, and quantifying their skills acquisition, I plead for the according of a higher priority to children's inner lives. I ask us to uphold their birthright to wonder and to question and to make up their own 'superheroes.' Let them experiment and be wrong but in their own terms so that is they who want to find better answers (this is how Socrates does it in the *Meno*). (p. 227)

Spitz's book contains examples of how the child's imagination can be nurtured in music, math, writing, and art.

Metaphor

Another tool for enhancing intuition is metaphor. Metaphorical thinking involves making connections between two words or ideas that are not normally related but which share some commonalty. For example, the human kidney is like a fuel filter in that both screen out certain molecules. Of course, there are significant differences between the fuel filter and the kidney, but a discussion of similarities and differences can lead to a more complete understanding of both. Other examples of the metaphor include the following: 'a revolution can be compared to a volcano (pressure building toward explosion), narrative writing to a chain with the transitions being the links, theme and variation to the Thanksgiving turkey and the endless ways of preparing its leftovers, and electricity to water running through pipes' (Williams, 1983, p. 56).

Metaphorical teaching asks students to explore connections and make intuitive leaps. W.J.J. Gordon (1966) has described different levels of role-taking that can take place in metaphorical thinking. At the first level the person merely describes an object by drawing out the obvious similarities between the two objects or ideas. At the next level the person describes emotions that arise from identifying the similarities. At the third level the student makes an empathetic identification with a living thing. Gordon (1966) gives the example of a student imagining herself as a crab:

O.K. I'm a fiddler crab. I've got armor all around me my tough shell. You'd think I could take it easy, but I can't. And that big claw of mine! Big deal! It looks like a great weapon, but it's a nuisance. I wave it around to scare everyone, but I can hardly carry it. Why can't I be big and fast and normal like other crabs? No kidding! That claw doesn't even scare anyone! (p. 24)

The fourth level involves empathetic identification with a non-living object.

There are several advantages to using metaphor. The most obvious, from a holistic perspective, is that it encourages the student to draw connections between ideas and subject matter. Williams's (1983) graph of metaphor (see figure 6.2) is congruent with the diagram of transformational learning given in figure 1.4. Here she shows the traditional approach, which can be compared to the transmission position, and the metaphorical approach, which is similar to the transformation, or holistic position. In the traditional approach seeds and eggs are seen as unrelated while in the holistic approach the intersecting circles represent the points where we can make connections.

Metaphor encourages the student not only to make connections but to see patterns. In comparing revolutions to volcanoes the student must

Figure 6.2 Metaphorical Teaching

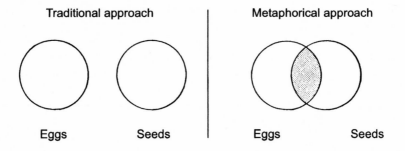

examine the patterns and principles common to both and then make the connection between the two. The most powerful connections between the components of a metaphor are not similar details but similar principles, as in the example of the kidney and the fuel filter. The student must understand the underlying function of each object to see the connection.

Another advantage of the metaphor is that it is open-ended and provokes inquiry. Metaphors by their very nature encourage questions since metaphoric inquiry rarely has ready-made answers. For example, in comparing X and Y we first have to inquire into the nature of each and then draw comparisons.

Wilson (2001) argues that metaphors are critical to the learning process and that teachers in working with elementary school children should use metaphorical language in their teaching. Steinbergh (1999) also explores the use of metaphor with elementary school children with a particular focus on poetry. She argues that poetry naturally lends itself to the use of metaphor, and the students' ability to use metaphor increases in complexity as they mature. She found that in the primary years metaphors tend to be very concrete and by early adolescence they become more abstract. Using Piaget's developmental framework, Flynn (1995) believes that metaphors are best used with students who have reached formal operations. Flynn argues that metaphors can help the student to recall and integrate new concepts. Fleckenstein (1995) works with community college students and describes methods of teaching student writers through the use of metaphor. She argues that these methods help students develop skills of imagination and logical reasoning.

Metaphors can sometimes be used at the beginning of a lesson to stimulate interest in the material. One teacher began his class on the French Revolution by examining the power structure of the school (Williams, 1983). Once the students saw how power functioned in their own institution they were then more interested in the power struggles in eighteenth-century France. Williams notes: 'Instead of memorizing the Three Estates and the roles each played, students looked for analogues in the school, explored the power relations between groups, and related them to the situation in France' (p. 69).

Metaphors can also be used in testing. Again, the answer to a metaphoric question on a test will not be scorable with a simple checklist, but instead the teacher will be asked to assess the student's reasoning and the connections that he or she draws. Below is an example:

1. List the major events leading up to the French Revolution and explain their importance.
2. How was the period leading up the French Revolution like the building up of a thunderstorm? Be sure to include in your analogy the major events leading up to the Revolution. (Williams, 1983, p. 71)

Metaphor can also be used to stimulate creative writing. The following questions are from Gordon's (1968) synectics approach:

1. What <u>MACHINE</u> acts like a <u>SPLINTER GOING INTO YOUR FINGER</u>? (p. 8)
2. How is a <u>BEAVER CHEWING ON A LOG</u> like a <u>TYPEWRITER</u>? (p. 8)
3. What <u>ANIMAL</u> is like a <u>PARACHUTE</u>? (p. 9)
4. What <u>THING IN THE KITCHEN</u> is like a <u>BEAVER</u>? (p. 9)

Metaphor can also be combined with imagery to encourage creative thinking. For example, Williams suggests the following activity in which the teacher begins by taking the students on a guided fantasy of a rose garden. The students visualize seeing, touching, and smelling the red rose. While their eyes are still closed the teacher then reads Robert Burns's poem 'My Love Is Like a Red, Red Rose.' After the reading, the students discuss the experience and how it might change with a different flower or even a different coloured rose.

Finally, metaphors can be used in teaching science. Russell Stannard (2001), who has written books such as *The Time and Space of Uncle Albert* and *Uncle Albert and the Quantum Quest*, believes that stories are a

good way to explain complex ideas in physics. In these stories he uses
dreams to explore central ideas in modern physics. He also refers to the
work of Gamow (1965), who wrote books featuring a character called
Mr Tompkins to explain physics concepts.

Integrating a Critical Perspective

Some holistic educators, such as Kathleen Kesson (1993), have argued
that tools such as visualization can be used in different ways. She
states that techniques such as visualization are neutral and can 'either
work to emancipate consciousness, sustain the status quo, or open us
up to ever more subtle forms of domination' (p. 103). Kesson argues
that holistic education must be infused with a more critical perspective that allows students to examine societal institutions, particularly
those institutions such as capitalism that tend to separate and oppress
people.

I agree with Kesson but also agree with Steiner's perspective that
such analysis is best done during adolescence when the natural critical and analytical abilities of the student begin to flower. A good example of such a curriculum can be found at Central Park East Secondary School (CPESS) in New York, where the curriculum tends to focus
on central themes and questions that allow for integration and critical
thinking. For example, in seventh and eighth grades, students study
contemporary political issues with an emphasis on U.S. history. Below
is a list of essential questions that drive student inquiry:

1. What is political power?
2. Who has it?
3. How did they get it?
4. How does power change hands?
5. What gives laws their power?
6. How do people respond to being deprived of power? (Wood, 1992, p.
   180)

Students and teachers can also add their own questions. For example,
when students were studying the 1988 U.S.election they added the following questions:

Does your vote count? How does one go about getting the agreement of
the majority of a country? Are voting blocs really blocs? How does the

media influence elections? How does one achieve political power? Is this the best way to choose a leader? (Wood, 1992, p. 180)

Literature is used to explore the central question of power in order to complement the historical investigation. For example, Steinbeck's novel *Of Mice and Men* is used to explore the issue of powerlessness.

The humanities and social sciences curriculum at CPESS also looks at different political systems around the world. Students look at concepts such as 'justice, fairness, conflict resolution' in terms of how the U.S. government and other countries address these issues. Essential questions include: 'How is authority justified? Who has it? How are conflicts resolved?' (Wood, 1992, p. 169). This curriculum also examines non-European traditions in selected Asian, Central American, and African countries. The curriculum focuses on clashes between non-Western and Western societies and ideas. The central focus here is on essential questions that help integrate the curriculum and address fundamental issues.

In Waldorf education students study the revolutions from different countries in grade 8 just as they begin to question authority in their own lives. However, this is done after a curriculum that has focused on the integration of the emotional life of the child from ages seven to eleven or twelve. Myth and story are used to help this process. As children develop a healthy sense of self, they are then ready to question and analyse the world around them.

Matt Copeland (2005), who teaches at Washburn Rural High School in Topeka, Kansas, advocates the use of *Socratic circles* in middle and high schools. Socratic circles consist of two circles: the inner circle discusses a text or question while the surrounding circle observes the discussion. During the discussion the outside circle just listens until the discussion is completed. Once the inner circle has completed the discussion the outer circle then gives the inner circle feedback. After the feedback is given the outer circle moves to the inner circle and the process is repeated. Copeland argues that Socratic circles develop the following skills:

- critical thinking and reflection, as students examine language and ideas more carefully
- creativity in writing
- the desire to read more, as the circles stimulate students to research a subject, which leads to further reading
- more confident speaking

- listening skills;
- team-building skills, which teach the students to respect other points of view
- conflict resolution

In summary, Socratic circles provide a forum that integrates both critical and creative thinking as well as important interpersonal skills.

Multiple Intelligences

The work of Howard Gardner (1983) provides a broader conception of human intelligence than has been used within most educational settings. His intelligences theory provides a framework for exploring various modes of thinking. The eight intelligences include: *linguistic* (language development, abstract reasoning, use of symbols); *logical/mathematical* (scientific thinking, use of abstract symbols, and recognizing patterns); *visual/spatial* (visual arts, architecture, imagery, visual discrimination); *bodily/kinesthetic* (sports activities, body movement and expression, dance); *musical* (perceiving and interpreting sound); *interpersonal* (working cooperatively with others, feeling empathy for others, responding to the needs of others); *intrapersonal* (awareness of internal states, intuition, and reflection); and *natural* (awareness of the environment).

Gardner's model has been applied on numerous occasions to the field of education. For example, the Pittsburgh Public Schools and the Educational Testing Service have collaborated with Gardner on a project called Arts PROPEL. This project has focused on assessment so as to move beyond what Gardner refers to as 'the often wooden standardized instruments' (1983, p. 238) that have been used so inappropriately in the arts. The project has also involved the development of a curriculum in the arts (Gardner, 1991). David Lazear (1991a, 1991b) has also applied Gardner's work to an educational setting. Lazear has developed a number of classroom activities that teachers can use to develop the various intelligences.

There is much to admire in Gardner's work and its application. However, I am concerned about his relating the different intelligences to different areas of the brain, which, as in the case of the right/left brain concept, leads to a reductionist approach to learning. I do not believe that all learning should be linked to areas of the brain.

As a complement to brain-based learning, I think we can also speak of a soul-based approach to learning (Moore, 1992; Miller, 2000). A soul-based approach realizes that some learning cannot be necessarily connected to a physiological place in the body but is characterized instead by paradox, spontaneity, and mystery. Through mechanistic approaches to curriculum and learning, such as standardized testing and outcomes-based education, we have taken the soul out of the curriculum. If Elizabeth Peabody was right when she wrote that 'education depends on its attitude towards soul' (as cited in Alcott, 1991, p. xvii), then much of our present approach to curriculum is simply misguided. By restoring intuition to the curriculum, we can begin to bring soul, life, and vitality back into the classroom.

References

Ainsworth-Land, V. (1982). Imagining and creativity: An integrating perspective. *The Journal of Creative Behavior, 16*, 5–28.

Alcott, A.B. (1991). *How like an angel came I down*. (A.O. Howell, Ed. & Intro.). Hudson, NY: Lindisfarne Press.

Arcavi, A. (2003). The role of visual representations in the learning of mathematics. *Educational studies in mathematics, 52*, 215–41.

Beyer, B.K. (1991). *Teaching thinking skills: A handbook for secondary school teachers*. Boston: Allyn & Bacon.

Bohm, D. (1984). Insight, knowledge, science and human values. In D. Sloan (Ed.), *Toward the recovery of wholeness* (pp. 8–30). New York: Teachers College Press.

Bugental, J. (1976). *The search for existential identity*. San Francisco: Jossey Bass.

Calvin, M. (1976, Fall). Dialogue: Your most exciting moment in research? *LBL Magazine*.

Chatterjea, K. (1999). Use of visual images in the teaching of geography. *Geographical education, 12*, 49–55.

Copeland, M. (2005). *Socratic circles: Fostering critical and creative thinking in middle and high schools*. Portland, ME: Stenhouse.

Eisenwine, M., Fowler, E., & McKenzie, G. (2000, Winter). Visual memory and context cues in reading instruction. *Journal of Curriculum and Supervision, 15*, 170–4.

Fleckenstein, K. (1995, May). Writing and the strategic use of metaphor. *Teaching English in the Two-Year College, 22*, 110–15.

Flynn, L. (1995, Winter). Learning concepts independently through metaphor. *Reading Improvement, 32*, 200–19.

Gaylean, B.C. (1983). *Mind sight: Learning through imaging*. Berkeley, CA: Center for Integrative Learning.

Gamow, G. (1965). *Mr. Tompkins in Paperback*. Cambridge: Cambridge University Press.

Gardner, H. (1983). *Frames of mind: The theory of multiple intelligences*. New York: Basic Books.

Gardner, H. (1991). *The unschooled mind: How children think and how schools should teach*. New York: Basic Books.

Gordon, W.J.J. (1966). *The metaphorical way of knowing*. Cambridge, MA: Porpoise Books.

Gordon, W.J.J. (1968). *Making it strange*. New York: Harper & Row.

Kesson, K. (1993). Critical theory and holistic education: Carrying on the conversation. In R. Miller (Ed.), *The renewal of meaning in education* (pp. 92–110). Brandon, VT: Holistic Education Press.

Lazear, D. (1991a). *Seven ways of knowing: Teaching for multiple intelligences*. Pallatine, IL: Skylight Publishing.

Lazear, D. (1991b). *Seven ways of teaching: The artistry of teaching with multiple intelligences*. Pallatine, IL: Skylight Publishing.

Miller, J.P. (1993). *The holistic teacher*. Toronto: OISE Press.

Miller, J.P. (2000). *Education and the soul: Toward a spiritual curriculum*. Albany, NY: SUNY Press.

Moore, T. (1992). *Care of the soul: A guide for cultivating depth and sacredness in everyday life*. New York: Walker.

Muller-Markus, S. (1976). The structure of creativity in physics. In E. Laszlo & E. Sellon (Eds.), *Vistas in physical reality*. New York: Selon Press.

Murdock, M. (1982). *Spinning inward: Using guided imagery with children*. Culver City, CA: Peace Press.

Murphy, M. (1992). *The future of the body: Explorations into the further evolution of human nature*. New York: Jeremy Tarcher.

Noddings, N., & Shore, P.J. (1984). *Awakening the inner eye: Intuition in education*. New York: Teachers College Press.

Pearson, M. (1998). *Emotional healing and self-esteem: Inner-life skills of relaxation, visualisation and meditation for children and adolescents*. Melbourne: Australian Council for Educational Research.

Richardson, A. (1969). *Mental imagery*. New York: Springer Publishing.

Ross, J., & Maynes, F. (1982). *Teaching problem solving*. Toronto: OISE Press.

Samuels, M., & Samuels, N. (1975). *Seeing with the mind's eye: The history, techniques and uses of visualization*. New York: Random House.

Simonton, C., & Matthews-Simonton, S. (1978). *Getting well again: A step-by-step guide to overcoming cancer for patients and their families*. Los Angeles: Tarcher.

Singer, J. (1976, July). Fantasy, the foundation of serenity. *Psychology Today.*

Spitz,. E.H. (2006). *The brigthening glance: Imagination and childhood.* New York: Pantheon.

Stannard, R. (2001, January). Communicating physics through story. *Physics Education, 36,* 30–4.

Steinbergh, J. (1999, March). Mastering metaphor through poetry. *Language arts, 76,* 231–4.

Teilhard de Chardin, P. (1965). *The phenomenon of man.* New York: Harper Torch Books.

Tart, C. (1975). The physical universe, the spiritual universe and the paranormal. In C. Tart (Ed.), *Transpersonal Psychologies* (pp. 115–51). New York: Harper & Row.

Vaughan, F. (1979). *Awakening intuition.* Garden City, NY: Anchor Books.

Wallas, G. (1926). *The art of thought.* London: Watts.

Weil, A. (1972). *The natural mind.* Boston: Houghton Mifflin.

Wheatley, G.H. (1998, Spring/Summer). Imagery and mathematics. *Focus on Learning Problems in Mathematics, 20,* 65–77.

Williams, L.V. (1983). *Teaching for the two-sided mind.* Englewood Cliffs, NJ: Prentice Hall.

Wilson, S.L.A. (2001). 'A metaphor is pinning air to the wall': A literature review of children's use of metaphor. *Childhood Education, 77*(2), 96–9.

Wood, G.H. (1992). *Schools that work: America's most innovative public education programs.* New York: Plume.

CHAPTER SEVEN

Body–Mind Connections

Wilder Penfield, the Canadian neurosurgeon and brain researcher, found that our awareness (the mind) is not located in any particular part of the brain but, in fact, directs the brain. According to Penfield (1975), our mind 'seems to focus attention. The mind is aware of what is going on. The mind reasons and makes new decisions. It understands, it acts as though endowed with an energy of its own, it can make decisions and put them into effect by calling upon various brain mechanisms' (p. 80). However, it is also possible for the brain to run on 'automatic pilot' without the conscious awareness of the mind. When this happens, the body–mind connection can be broken.

James Lynch (1985) has studied the relation between mind and body and has found that many people suffering from hypertension (high blood pressure) are not aware of their body messages. For example, when their heart is beating at a high rate, they will not be conscious of their heart pounding. Lynch also found that people who suffer from migraines often experience a drop in blood pressure and have cold hands before the onset of a migraine; however, the patient is often unaware of these bodily changes.

According to Lynch, hypertension is a major health problem in the United States, affecting between 40 to 60 million Americans. In his studies, Lynch has found that one of the main reasons for the disease is that people with high blood pressure have lost touch with their bodies. The hypertensive's mind does not hear the messages (e.g., muscle tension) the body is sending.

Lynch's study found that blood pressure tends to rise markedly while the subject is talking. Hypertensive patients also have a hard time listening, as they are preoccupied with what they will be saying next. Lynch found that human dialogue is characterized by a rhythm of increased heartbeat and blood pressure while talking and lower heartbeat and blood pressure while listening. This coincides with the model of the active-ego-based mind and the listening-soul-based mind. Often in talking we are trying to persuade, to manipulate, and to bring the other person in line with the ego's view. While listening, we are less likely to be planning and manipulating; but instead simply relating to the world as it is.

Other researchers have arrived at similar conclusions: that the psychosomatic patient (those who experience physical symptoms that have mental or emotional causes) is not in touch with his or her body and feelings. For example, Freedman and Sweet (1954) use the term 'emotional illiterates' to describe psychosomatic patients who have a difficult time describing their feelings. These patients became bewildered when it was suggested that emotional problems may be contributing to their physical problems. Friedman and Sweet concluded that psychosomatics bury their emotional problems in their bodies so deeply that they lose their capacity for insight. In other words, they are running on automatic pilot and their conscious awareness is no longer in touch with their bodies and feelings.

Two French psychiatrists, Marty and de M'Uzan (1963), published a paper showing that psychosomatic patients displayed a paucity of feeling when describing their difficulties as well as a lack of fantasy. Marty and de M'Uzan referred to psychosomatics' responses to questions about their feelings as 'operational thinking.' They also noted that these patients did not relate their feelings to changes in their bodies but tended to focus on small, trivial details of external events. For example, the normal patient, when asked, 'How do you know you were angry?' will describe their stomach churning or their muscles becoming tense, while the psychosomatic refers to external events.

Building on the work of these investigators, Peter Sifneos (1975) coined the term *alexithymia* to describe the fact that psychosomatic patients are not able to describe their feelings. In another study on alexithymia, Krystal (1979) found that these patients showed a marked impairment in their capacity for creativity and their ability to fantasize. Krystal's research seems to support Singer's research described in the last chapter which indicates that imagination is important to the development of wholeness.

In summarizing this research, Lynch concludes that psychosomatic patients seal themselves off from others, or from what Lynch calls the social membrane. For Lynch real speech involves an invitation of the speaker to enter into his or her consciousness – 'that is, into his or her body and ultimately into his or her mind's heart' (1985, p. 243). For the psychosomatic, this invitation becomes a threat, as 'their speech becomes an act of battering or hiding, rather than an invitation' (1985, p. 243).

Lynch argues that there are two primary reasons for the modern problem of hypertension and particularly the large number of psychosomatics who are cut off from their feelings and their bodies. One is the seventeenth-century movement led by French mathematician and philosopher René Descartes that tended to see the person as a soul trapped in a machine. According to Lynch (1985),

> Descartes removed the Greek idea of logos from living bodies and limited it to a soul that was restricted to the human mind. By separating soul from body, Descartes, in essence, created two realities for humans; one, a machine body; and the other, a mind or soul which interacts both with the machine body as well as with other human beings. Thus, human beings relate to each other in dialogue only through their minds. (pp. 289–90).

Lynch notes that it was significant that Descartes's fundamental statement was 'I think therefore I am' rather than 'I feel therefore I am.' If we relate to each other only through our minds, then human dialogue becomes strictly rational dialogue. According to Lynch, 'in this new view, the feeling of love is merely an imprecise thought; loneliness has nothing to do with physical health ... Descartes made the human body utterly irrelevant to human dialogue' (p. 291).

Abram (1996) also points to Descartes's work as contributing to our alienation from the body. He believes this has led to our disconnection from the environment, as the body and the earth are intimately connected. Indigenous people have made this connection. Abrams describes how the native peoples of Australia would walk the routes of their ancestors, and in this process the body and the land would become one. Abram states: 'he virtually *becomes* the journeying Ancestor, and thus the storied earth is born afresh' (p. 170).

Abram also refers to the French philosopher Maurice Merleau-Ponty as someone who saw the connection between the body and the land. Referring to Merleau-Ponty's concept of language, he writes:

> The complex interchange that we call 'language' is rooted in the non-ver-

bal exchange always already going on between our own flesh and the flesh of the world ... Experientially considered, language is no more the special property of the human organism than it is an expression of the animate earth that enfolds us. (p. 90)

Another reason for body–mind divisions is our educational system. Lynch argues that school systems emphasize calculus and physics, which require a great deal of training, while feelings are taken for granted. There is 'no training, no exercising, no sensitizing – except, that is, for a rational discussion of these human feelings' (p. 271). Lynch concludes:

For many students, school systems can become a training ground where they are taught not to understand but rather to control their feelings. For those individuals who are already predisposed to be particularly insensitive to their feelings, and who will subject themselves later in life to serious psychosomatic disorders, the entire experience in schools serves to reinforce their problems. Feelings are seen as an irrational force, a dark side of human nature that must be controlled. The academic lesson is that if you cannot control your feelings, then at least you ought to hide them. Since those attitudes and beliefs coincide with and amplify similar parental dispositions, psychosomatically prone individuals often do well in school. Not sensing feelings and compulsively following structure and rules is precisely the type of behavior that prepares one to do well on objective tests. It allows one to spend endless hours learning minute details from texts while simultaneously denying one's anxiety and anger at having to spend so much time competing with fellow students. (p. 271)

Masters and Houston (1978) come to a similar conclusion when they claim that school leads to inadequate development of the body. They cite the research of Wilfred Barlow, which indicates that most children have a number of physical defects that increase as they grow older. Barlow (1975), who conducted his research in secondary schools and colleges in England, reached the following conclusions:

Seventy percent of all boys and girls show quite marked muscular and postural deficiencies. Mostly these defects appear as passing inefficiencies and difficulties in learning; they become accentuated in emotional situations, and they presage an uneasy adolescence in which childhood faults become blown up into full-fledged defects. By the age of eighteen, only

5 percent of the population are free from defects, 15 percent have slight defects, 65 percent have quite severe defects, and 15 percent have very severe defects. These figures are based on my published surveys of boys and girls from secondary schools, and students from physical training, music and drama colleges, some of whom might reasonably be expected to have a higher physical standard than the rest of the population. (p. 15)

We have no reason to believe these figures would be any different in North America. Even physical education programs which are aimed at developing the body can contribute to a lack of integration. Masters and Houston believe that physical exercises should concentrate on developing a person's body image or the ability to connect the body to our consciousness. Unfortunately, many physical education programs focus only on building up the muscles and the cardiovascular system. Masters and Houston conclude that exercises such as 'running and jogging, weightlifting, rope-skipping, swimming, isometrics, isotonics, and sports in general can, in fact, be detrimental' (p. 36). Shelton (1971) agrees:

There is hardly any form of athletics in which all of the muscles are not brought into play, but when we study their activities we see that some parts of the body are taxed sufficiently to produce considerable development while others are only slightly used. Marvelous control is required in some parts to execute the movements, while others require little or no control. Every game or sport exercises and develops some groups of muscles or some region of the body more than other groups or regions and in time produces more or less deformity if not counter-balanced by other features of the exercise program. The unevenness in the distribution of effort results in uneven development and control. The result is that our athletes are miserable specimens. (p. 37)

The competitive aspect of sports often causes athletes to overtrain or develop certain parts of their bodies at the expense of the whole body. For example, baseball players lift weights so they can hit more home runs, resulting in muscle rib cage injuries. Two sports often thought to be beneficial are swimming and cycling. However, Bertherat and Bernstein (1977) note that swimming can lead to overdeveloped back muscles while the front of the body can remain undeveloped. They also conclude that a common effect of cycling is a 'tightening of the muscles in the back of the neck and lower back; on the other hand, a loss of tonicity in the abdominal muscles and a compression of the stomach ... can lead to digestive problems (very common in professional cyclists)' (pp. 58–9).

Psychophysical Re-education

Masters and Houston (1978) offer a program in psychophysical aware-ness. This is a program based in part on the work of Frederick M. Al-exander and Moshe Feldenkrais and attempts to connect 'words and images to the appropriate movements and sensations' (p. 61). The exercises focus on different parts of the body and include an imagery component to help connect mind and body. The Alexander technique and the Feldenkrais system of functional integration are based on the premise that the body and the nervous system are closely connected. Problems can arise because the body can get the wrong messages from the nervous system. Feldenkrais (1970), however, argues that the body can be re-educated:

> Many of our failings, physical and mental, need not therefore be consid-ered as diseases to be cured, nor an unfortunate trait of character, for they are neither. They are an acquired result of a learned faulty mode of doing. The body only executes what the nervous system makes it do. It moulds it-self during growth for a longer period, and to a greater extent, than in any other animal. Actions repeated innumerable times for years on end, such as all our habitual actions, mould even the bones, let alone the muscular envelope. The physical faults that appear in our body long after we were born are mainly the result of activity we have imposed on it. Faulty modes of standing and walking produce flat feet, and it is the mode of standing and walking that must be corrected, and not the feet. The extent to which our frame is able to adjust itself to the use and requirements we make of it seems to be limitless; by learning a better use of control, the feet, the eyes, or whatever organ it may be, will again adjust themselves and change their shape and function accordingly. The transformations that can be pro-duced, and their rapidity, sometimes border on the incredible. (p. 152)

According to Master and Houston, the re-education of the body must start in the motor cortex of the brain. They suggest that when a person's wrist is broken there may occur an inhibition in the motor cortex. This inhibition occurs as a result of the inactivity since the wrist is in a cast or splints. When the cast is removed it may be difficult to move the wrist because of the inhibition in the motor cortex. Masters and Houston suggest that mental exercises could help re-educate the brain so that the accompanying muscle activities can occur more easily. They claim that psychophysical re-education is

neural reeducation which makes the nervous system demonstrably more responsive and amenable to change. Psychophysical exercises are in part effective communications to the brain, specifying bodily changes which the brain can and will effect in response to the appropriate stimulus. (Masters & Houston, 1978, p. 49)

The following is a segment from one of the introductory exercises in the book:

Put your arms down at your sides with the palms of your hands down. And just imagine turning your head from left to right. Imagine it vividly, what it feels like, how far the head goes to each side, and how quickly you do it. Imagine that you fold your arms over your chest and continue to imagine turning the head. Imagine that at least ten times, taking care that you breathe freely as you do it. When you imagined the movement with the arms folded over the chest, did you imagine that the shoulders and the back left the floor? ... Now with your eyes open, actually turn your head quickly from side to side. Notice whether your shoulders go up and down as the head turns, and do so spontaneously. Then stop, rest, and close your eyes. (pp. 97–8)

Psychophysical re-education, then, combines visualization with movement to enhance physical performance and well-being.

Mindfulness

Another technique for connecting mind and body is awareness of movement. When we focus on moment-to-moment awareness, this is called mindfulness. Mindfulness, however, has become difficult to achieve in today's modern industrialized society. With television, Internet, and music at home or at work, we find our attention distracted. We often feel compelled to do two or three things at once. An example of this behaviour is the person who drives a car while talking on a cell phone, listening to the radio, and drinking coffee.

In contrast, mindfulness encourages us to slow down and focus on one task at a time. If we are doing the dishes, we are present with the soap, water, and the dishes and not ruminating over some problem. When we go for a mindful walk we are aware of our bodily movement, the air we breathe, and our surrounding environment. By being mindful we develop a connectedness with our body. After practice, the awareness becomes natural, even effortless. Mindfulness lets us become aware of any tension in the body almost immediately. By focusing attention on the stressful area in the body, one can relax the affected area so that tension does not build up in the body. Often we let tension build up in such areas as the neck and shoulders without being aware of the stress, and this can eventually affect how we feel and act. However, mindfulness lets us deal with tension almost immediately as it arises in the body. Mindfulness can be applied to all our movements, and other exercises can easily be developed with other activities (e.g., eating, swimming, writing). Below are two exercises from Hanh's (1976) *The Miracle of Mindfulness* that show how mindfulness can be applied to daily life:

Mindfulness while making tea
Prepare a pot of tea to serve a guest or to drink by yourself.

Do each movement slowly, in mindfulness. Do not let one detail of your movements go by without being mindful of it. Know that your hand lifts the pot by its handle. Know that you are pouring the fragrant warm tea into the cup. Follow each step in mindfulness. Breathe gently and more deeply than usual. Take hold of your breath if your mind strays.

Washing the dishes
Wash the dishes relaxingly, as though each bowl is an object of contemplation. Consider each bowl as sacred. Follow your breath to prevent your mind from straying. Do not try to hurry to get the job over with. Consider washing the dishes the most important thing in life. Washing the dishes is meditation. If you cannot wash the dishes in mindfulness, neither can you meditate while sitting in silence. (p. 85)

Jon Kabat-Zinn (2005) has introduced mindfulness into the medical profession with positive results. I have also conducted qualitative research on the effects of mindfulness training on teachers (Miller & Nozawa, 2002). Below is an example of how one teacher incorporated mindfulness into her teaching day:

I began each day marveling at the miracle of life, of falling asleep and awakening to a wondrous world. With this thought, I began my morning rituals. Thinking of my daily routines as rituals actually helped me in attaining a more aware state as I washed my face, took my shower, ate my breakfast and walked (or drove) to work. Upon entering the school, I decided to go to my classroom first. I had previously been going into the office to sign in and say good morning, etc. but this took away from the oneness that I needed in my 'mindfulness' training. I ritualized all my tasks – walking up the stairs, putting the key into the classroom door, hanging up my coat etc. It was actually amazing how being mindful of these simple tasks allowed me to begin my day in a calm, clear and less cluttered way. How many times had I come into this room, dumped my coat, hat and mitts on my chair, ran to the photocopy room and back, spent another half hour looking for the photocopying I had laid down somewhere, not to mention the frantic search for mitts when it was time go out on duty? Instead, I began to become aware of my mornings in the classroom and in turn they became calm and focussed.

My most favorite part of this pre-school ritual is writing the schedule on the board. My team teacher had tried to talk me out of this last June (she writes the daily schedule for each day on the sheets of chart paper and laminates them). At the time, I explained to her that writing of the schedule on the board had many different purposes for me. The most important one was that it allowed me to center myself in the classroom. I look back now on how intuitive I had been and I am amazed. Being mindful of this particular ritual has made me fully aware of the 'here' during the hectic day. I stand at the front of the room and feel the smooth texture of the chalk in my hands. I think about where I am and I observe my surroundings – the plants, the books, the desks, the children's slippers – I am, for the second time that day, amazed at the miracle of life.

The days begins, I stand outside the classroom fully aware of each individual as they enter the room. I interact with them, I say hello, it feels good. This is new; until now, I had never made it to the door when the children entered – I was always too busy! I try to maintain this sense of awareness – aware of my feelings (physical and emotional) and my reactions to the things that are happening 'now.' Of course, the craziness of the classroom day begins and it becomes more and more difficult to maintain this awareness as the day wears on. However, now instead of working through recess, I take the time to visit with colleagues in the staff room.

When I can, I take a walk down to the beach at lunch and look out across the lake, mindful of the beauty of the world around me. When the day ends, I recapture this mindful state and fully participate in the end-of-day ritual with my students. After the children have left, I sweep the floor, being mindful of my movements and the sound of the broom. I often begin by thinking that I am sweeping the days events away and that I am focusing on the 'now' – the actual act of sweeping. The pleasure of being here, and being able to fully participate reminds me again of the miracle of life. (Miller, 2006, p. 79–80)

Yoga

One of the biggest changes in the school system since the previous editions of *The Holistic Curriculum* were published has been the increasing use of yoga in schools. This reflects the growing popularity of yoga in North American culture. Several books have been published to introduce yoga to children and adolescents (Kiss, 2003; Lark, 2003; Luby, 2000; Schwartz, 2003). For young children in kindergarten and primary school, I still recommend Rachel Carr's *Be a Frog, a Bird, or a Tree: Creative Yoga Exercises for Children* (1973). Carr states that yoga exercises began in India when people tried to imitate the movements of animals and insects to increase the strength and flexibility in their own bodies. Carr began teaching yoga to young children in her own home. Gradually more and more children came, and her work led to her book. She found that her approach also stimulated the childrens' imaginations:

When they learned to balance in the frog pose, they felt the need for continued motion and so organized frog races, croaking as they hopped with quick well-co-ordinated movements. This led to further imaginative play. The more agile children arched their back high up so that others could crawl under them. (p. 79)

Carr found that the children could help one another learn the poses. She also worked with children with various physical disabilities and describes an incident of how one child helped another:

When one boy in the group found the pose of the tree too confusing, tears sprang to his eyes. His jerky, unco-ordinated movements frustrated him. Rushing to his aid was a lithe youngster whose hearing and speech were so impaired that he communicated only in sign language. He gently led his friend to a wall for support, then moved the boy's trembling limbs into the pose of the tree. The triumph brought spontaneous applause from the entire group. (p. 80)

Using the images of animals helped the children remember the poses over time. Carr used a circle to teach the poses and had one child in the middle demonstrating the pose to the rest of the circle. She also suggests basic guidelines for doing the exercises such as not doing them right after a meal and wearing loose, flexible clothing.

One student in my class, Nancy Zigrovic (2005), teaches at a secondary school in Oakville, Ontario, and uses both meditation and yoga with her students. She describes her experience with one class:

I have also had the pleasure to work with a Grade 10 Applied Canadian History class of 20 students, 14 of whom are boys. Many of these students provide the quintessential example of discouraged learners – they are adolescents who often find the traditional classroom a very difficult place to be. They find it hard to focus and listen attentively, and are often described by teachers as 'behavioural problems.' However, from the first time that we tried both meditation and yoga together, they were receptive and open to new approaches. In our meditation, we began with short exercises in breathing and focus. They seemed at first reluctant to close their eyes in the presence of their peers; I explained that they could simply gaze downwards in front of them. When they could see that I felt comfortable in the classroom and had closed my eyes, all began to follow what I was modelling. Even in our first debriefing, they talked about how they liked being still for a few moments.

During my next and subsequent visits with the History class, we moved into a more physical form of hatha yoga, incorporating what we had already learned about breathing and focus. One of the initial responses from a boy in the class included, 'I thought that this yoga was pretty good. If we did it a little longer, it would probably be better. And once we get past the stage of laughing it would be good.' We did work at sustaining our practice for longer periods of time and the students became more comfortable with the various asanas as well as with making space for silence. Most importantly, however, they began to trust each other, and the hurtful comments that seemed to be a regular part of the classroom vernacular were becoming less frequent. In their latest reflection, not one student expressed concern about doing yoga or wished to not participate in the practice. I have been meeting with this particular class two times per week during the past two months, and some of their comments include:

At first when we were doing it, I didn't think it would really work, but after doing the exercises, I felt really relaxed and good. My favourite one would be the Namaste. It really makes me stretch and relieve stress. Thank-you for doing it with us.

Another student wrote:

I like the yoga because it helps me concentrate a lot better because usually I can't concentrate very well. It also helps me calm down and focus on what I am doing.

And this student summarizes the soul connection:

This isn't the first time I've done yoga. We had to do this for hockey, before our championship game, our coach's wife used to be a yoga instructor. We ended up winning the championship game because we were all refreshed from our little yoga session. My opinion on yoga is it soothes the soul. (pp. 9–10)

Movement and Dance

Another vehicle for connecting mind and body is movement and dance. Movement education became more popular in the late 1960s and 1970s, particularly in primary level classrooms. One of the greatest teachers and performers of movement and dance in the twentieth century was Isadora Duncan, whose approach to movement is outlined in a recent biography by Fredericka Blair (1986). Isadora was critical of dance that focused on technique unconnected to inner feeling. She wrote in her book *The Art of Dance* of 'those systems of dancing that are only arranged gymnastics, only too logically understood (Dalcroze, etc.)' (Blair, 1986, p. 51). Instead, she taught her pupils, 'Remember always start your movements from within. The desire to make a certain gesture must be there first' (as cited in Irma Duncan, n.d., p. 12).

Isadora focused on natural movements such as walking, running, and skipping, always attempting to connect the outward movement to the inner feeling. To her, the goal of dance was not expression of personal feeling as much as the expression of universal feelings, coming from the dancer's deepest emotion. The dancer's body

is simply the luminous manifestation of his soul ... This is the truly creative dancer, natural but not imitative, speaking in movement out of himself and out of something greater than all selves. (Isadora Duncan, 1928, p. 52)

Isadora did not deny technique but stressed that it must be integrated with this universal sense. She realized that the dancer must work so that he or she passes through 'stages of psychological and physical self-awareness to reach this final stage of self-forgetfulness, of surrendering to the music and the promptings of one's innermost being' (Blair, 1986, p. 49). In sum, Isadora offered a holistic approach to dance that should be considered by educators when developing movement programs.

Dimonstein (1971) has developed a holistic approach to dance for the elementary classroom. The focus of her approach is on developing kinesthetic awareness. Kinesthetic awareness refers to children's ability to control their movements and to feel the movements at the same time. With gestures they learn to give shape and form to their inner thoughts. Dance, then, is not just acting out, but giving form to inner feelings through visual images expressed through movement. For example, in exploring the concept of fear, the children find some movement to express their conception of fear. The students can first start with an unstructured visualization in which they let images of fear come into their minds. They then can articulate these images or draw them, and finally they can express their image of fear through movement.

Dimonstein describes three stages of movement and dance. At the first stage the students explore their physical self with basic movement patterns. The next level is improvisation, in which students begin to connect inner feelings with movement. At this level they begin to use movement as a form of self-expression, although the students usually have not yet reached the level of dance in which there is definite form to the movements.

At the dance level, children deepen their perception of inner feelings by giving shape to them through physical activity. In dance there is movement into patterns that express a particular idea or theme. For Dimonstein (1971), however, dance is not storytelling. Instead, it focuses on 'metaphoric qualities which symbolize forces or objects' (p. 13). The body is the centre in this symbolic process. Through dance children develop 'muscle sense' or kinesthetic perception of bodily movement. In dance they gain a sense of flow and rhythm, as movement is not isolated but part of a whole. While dancing, the children develop a sense of fluency, as their bodies become more centred. As the children gain this 'muscle sense' they learn to express their own feelings and they also learn which movement is appropriate. Dance, then, becomes a vehicle for expressing the inner life of the child.

An excellent source of movement/dance experiences can be found in Teresa Benzwie's *A Moving Experience: Dance for Lovers of Children and the Child Within* (1987). Focusing on the elementary school children, she suggests activities in the following areas: range, space, rhythm, name games, language, communication, movement games and warm ups, sculpting, art and movement, music and movement, fantasy, and props.

Ellen Spitz (2006) describes how young children's movements can reflect the environment they are in. She describes the movement of a six-year-old girl, Alla, at the Guggenheim Museum. She has just completed climbing to the top of the museum with her mother:

> Little Alla now begins to do something quite surprising. Keeping her body as close to the railing, she starts spinning round and round as she slowly descends the ramp. Why is she doing this? What is she thinking? Watching her in puzzlement, her mother takes just a few moments to realize that, with the movements of her own body, the little girl is now recapitulating her kinesthetic experience of the entire architectural space created by Frank Lloyd Wright in the museum's interior. Round and round she twirls until her mother asks her gently to be careful so that she won't become dizzy and fall down. (p. 37)

Waldorf Education and Eurythmy

Rudolf Steiner, the Austrian philosopher who investigated and developed approaches to so many areas of human endeavour such as farming, architecture, and medicine, is also known for developing Waldorf education. The Waldorf movement, which began in 1919, has become the fastest-growing independent school movement in the world. Steiner based his pedagogy on his conception of the human being. This conception led to an emphasis on his particular form of movement – eurythmy.

Eurythmy is used at all levels of Waldorf education, although it is probably most important during the elementary years. Eurythmy is not dance movement or personal expression; instead, it is a physical form of speech. The physical gestures are taken from the movements of the larynx. The arms and hands are very important in eurythmy. Eurythmy can also be performed to music, and this is called 'tone eurythmy.' When I was at the Waldorf school, grade 4 students were doing tone eurythmy by moving to major and minor chords.

In the early grades the children walk and run to form geometrical forms such as circles, figure eights, squares, triangles, and pentagons.

Eurythmy can help the unsocial child learn how to move in time with the other children and can teach the overintellectual child to step in time to rhythm. Eurythmy can also be combined with storytelling at the primary grades. Harwood (1958) comments:

> If we are going to perform a little story in this sort of eurythmic action, music must also come in. The children begin to feel the qualities of different rhythms – perhaps the light anapest for the prince's horse galloping through the forest – the trochee for the princess lost at night in that same forest and thinking of the home she will never see again – the spondee for the ogre walking heavily home from his day's marauding. Picture, rhythm and feeling – when these are a unity and realized in movement, education has begun. (p. 151)

Older children can try more complicated movements such as marking the beat with the feet while clapping the rhythm with hands and then reversing the process. Eurythmy can also be practised with rods so that if the movement is not done correctly the student's rod will clash with a neighbour's rod. These exercises, then, develop both control of the body and concentration. As the children in grades 4 and 5 study history, myth, and legends, they can apply their learning to eurythmy. The rhythm of the Norse legends can be compared to Greek mythology. Harwood notes that the 'alliterative meter of the North has a deep quality of will in it ... while the hexameter on the other hand, is the most harmonious, the most harmonizing of all rhythms' (p. 152). By reading Homer and then doing eurythmy the students gain a much deeper feel for Greek culture than they could through a mere verbal approach.

As the child approaches adolescence, eurythmy can be related to the intellectual development of the student. For example, grammar can be explored through eurythmy as the active and passive tense are taught through movement. Students at this age can relate more closely to music and eurythmy by having some students play their instruments while the other students do some movements.

Eurythmy is usually taught by a teacher trained in the field, but the classroom teacher is encouraged to take part in the lesson. According to Harwood, 'when the eurythmy teacher is as much interested in what the children are learning in their main lessons, as the class teacher in what they are doing in movement, the children thrive in a harmony of mind and will' (p. 154). In secondary school, eurythmy can be combined with drama, 'perhaps in a play when there are nature spirits, as in Milton's *Comus*, or *A Midsummer Night's Dream*' (p. 155). Harwood concludes by emphasizing the importance of eurythmy in Waldorf education:

> Of all elements in modern life it is the rhythmical side which is most deficient – a deficiency only too apparent in the arts today. The whole of a Waldorf education is based on rhythm, and may therefore be called curative for an age. But in this rhythmical education there is no doubt where the centre lies. It is in Eurythmy. (p. 155)

Drama in Education (Dorothy Heathcote)

The English educator Dorothy Heathcote has developed a transformational approach to drama. This approach is called *drama in education* or *process drama*. Her approach focuses on problem solving or living through a particular moment in time rather than story or character development. Students use drama to 'explore the world in which a novel is set, to understand a historical event, to experience conflicts between different cultural groups, to see what other walks of life feel like' (Wagner, 1999, p. 1). Heathcote has used her approach in a variety of settings, from primary school to the university classroom. She has also worked with various occupational groups such as nurses or police officers and has taught individuals with various challenges and difficulties. Wagner (1999) summarizes her educational approach:

> Heathcote does not use children to produce plays. Instead, she uses drama to expand their awareness, to enable them to look at reality through fantasy, to see below the surface of actions to their meaning ... She does this not by heaping more information on them but by enabling them to use what they already know. (p. 3)

Heathcote is interested in helping classroom teachers, not drama specialists, to employ her methods. Her approach has been compared to the process of mental rehearsal where we work with a difficult problem or a new situation that is making us anxious. It can also be used to accept an experience that has been disturbing or traumatic.

Wagner used Heathcote's approach when she worked with a group of twelve- and thirteen-year-olds in Evanston, Illinois, who performed in front of an audience of adults at Northwestern University. The students decided to do a play about a ship at sea in 1610. They named the ship *The Dreamer*. She put one chair facing away from the group and had one child sit there. She asked them to imagine him as the ship's figurehead and said 'Look at him carefully. He is the Dreamer; he's supposed at this moment to be in wood. Stand there till you know he's in wood' (p. 5). She then told the students that the ship was being pulled out to sea by small boats and asked them to imagine how they feel as crew members about to go out to sea. After the students thought about this for moment, she asked them to go into the audience of adults and share their thoughts, which the adults then wrote down. The ideas then were read back to the children without identifying who said what. Some of the thoughts included the following:

> 'I'm afraid I'll never get off this ship.'
> 'It is strange to look at the figurehead up there because he seems to represent the whole crew.'
> 'I'm very scared. I'm not sure whether I'm ever going to see the town again. It's very exciting, and yet ... and yet ... I'm scared.'
> 'There's a feeling of mystery, wondering what the voyage will lead to.'
> 'We all have a dream, the dream of our own. It could be dangerous, things we might encounter on the water. We're scared, but we also dream of the riches and glory that we might achieve through discovery.' (p. 7)

Heathcote then turned to the student who is captain and said 'That is your crew.' This is a moment of reflection. Wagner suggests that no summary is needed because the students have captured the universal experience of embarking on the unknown. Heathcote relies on non-verbal awareness through the use of silent moments in which the student can just be with the experience. Wagner comments: 'The great advantage of a nonverbal approach is that it stays at the universal level of understanding. It introduces a class to holistic human experience that words haven't broken up' (p. 163). Heathcote likes to move back and forth between the verbal and non-verbal and not focus completely on one to the exclusion of the other.

Summary

By exploring psychophysical re-education, movement, dance, mindfulness, eurythmy, yoga, and drama we can help the student connect mind and body. By connecting mind and body we facilitate human wholeness. An example is the way James Lynch (1985), unlike the psychosomatic, listens to a fellow human being:

> At times I have found myself trembling when meeting the eyes of a patient – looking at me, searching, hoping earnestly to discover for the first time the emotional meaning of his or her elevated blood pressure, rapid heart rate, or freezing hands. At such moments I have felt Schrodinger's reality – deeply felt it – for surely there is far more to their eyes than optical sensors whose only function is to detect light quanta. And I have trembled then precisely because I have caught a glimpse of the infinite universe behind those eyes and the reality of a universal Logos uniting us in dialogue. And it is at such moments, in the quiet sharing of reason and feelings in dialogue, that I have felt most alive and human. (p. 310)

References

Abram, D. (1996). *The spell of the sensuous*. New York: Vintage.

Alexander, F.M. (1969). *The resurrection of the body*. New York: Delta Books.

Barlow, W. (1975). *The Alexander principle*. London: Arrow Books.

Benzwie, T. (1987). *A moving experience: Dance for lovers of children and the child within*. Tucson, AZ: Zephyr Press.

Bertherat, T., & Bernstein, C. (1977). *The body has its reasons: Anti-exercises and self-awareness*. New York: Pantheon Books.

Blair, F. (1986). *Isadora: Portrait of the artist as a woman*. New York: William Morrow.

Carr, R. (1973). *Be a frog, a bird, or a tree: Creative yoga exercises for children*. New York: Harper.

Dimonstein, G. (1971). *Children dance in the classroom*. New York: Macmillan.

Duncan, Irma. (n d.). *The technique of Isadora Duncan*. New York: Kamin.

Duncan, Isadora. (1928). *The art of dance*. (S. Cheney, Ed.). New York: Theatre Arts.

Feldenkrais, M. (1970). *Body and mature behavior*. New York: International Universities Press.

Feldenkrais, M. (1972). *Awareness through movement: Health exercises for personal growth*. New York: Harper & Row.

Freedman, M.B., & Sweet, B.S. (1954). Some specific features of group psychotherapy and their implications for selected patients. *International Journal of Group Psychotherapy, 4*, 355–68.

Hanh, T.N. (1976). *The miracle of mindfulness! A manual on meditation*. Boston: Beacon Press.

Harwood, A.C. (1958). *The recovery of man in childhood: A study in the educational work of Rudolf Steiner*. Spring Valley, NY: Anthroposophic Press.

Kabat-Zinn, J. (2005). *Coming to our senses: Healing ourselves and the world through mindfulness*. New York: Hyperion.

Kiss, M. (2003). *Yoga for young people*. New York: Sterling.

Krystal, H. (1979). Alexithymia and psychotherapy. *American Journal of Psychotherapy, 33*, 17–31.

Lark, L. (2003). *Yoga: Essential poses to help young people get fit, flexible, supple and healthy*. New York: Sterling.

Luby, T. (2000). *Yoga for teens*. Santa Fe, NM: Clear Light Publishers.

Lynch, J.J. (1985). *The language of the heart: The human body in dialogue*. New York: Basic.

Marty, P., & de M'Uzan, M. (1963). La pensée opératoire. *Revue Français Psychoanalysis, 27* (supplement): 1345.

Masters, R., & Houston, J. (1978). *Listening to the body: The psychophysical way to health and awareness*. New York: Dell/Delta.

Miller, J. (2006). *Educating for wisdom and compassion: Creating conditions for timeless learning*. Thousand Oaks, CA: Corwin.

Miller, J., & Nozawa, A. (2002). Meditating teachers: A qualitative study. *Journal of In-Service Education, 28*(1), 179–92.

Penfield, W. (1975). *The mystery of the mind: A critical study of consciousness and the human brain*. Princeton: Princeton University Press.

Schwartz, E. (2003). *I love yoga: A guide for kids and teens*. Toronto: Tundra Books.

Shelton, H.M. (1971). *Exercise!* Chicago: Natural Hygiene Press.

Sifneos, P.E. (1975). Problems of psychotherapy of patients with alexithymic characteristics and physical disease. *Psychotherapeutics and Psychosomatics, 26*, 68.

Spitz, E.H. (2006). *The brightening glance: Imagination and childhood*. New York: Pantheon.

Wagner, B.J. (1999). *Dorothy Heathcote: Drama as learning medium*. Portland: Calender Islands.

Zigrovic, N. (2005). *Journey towards spirituality*. Unpublished manuscript.

CHAPTER EIGHT

Subject Connections

Subjects have traditionally been at the heart of schooling. In the transmission curriculum they become central as subject matter can be taught in a manner unrelated to the needs and interests of students. In the holistic curriculum we attempt to make a number of connections with subject matter. One of the most important is between self and subject. If we can relate subject matter to the inner life of the child, subjects become less abstract and more relevant. It is also important to explore connections between subjects; this can be done through various integrated approaches to curriculum as well as through holistic-thinking models. Finally, subjects can connect the self to society. In this chapter we explore all of these connections.

Self and Subject

We have already touched on self and subject matter in Chapter 6 when we looked at visualization. Some of the guided imagery exercises can motivate student interest as well as develop student understanding. Perhaps one of the best examples of connecting self and subject comes from the work of Sylvia Ashton-Warner in her book *Teacher*. Ashton-Warner (1964) acknowledges that her approach is not new as she cites the work of Tolstoy and Anne Sullivan, the teacher of Helen Keller. For Ashton-Warner organic reading is 'the bridge from the known to the unknown; from the native culture to a new; and universally speaking, from the inner man out' (p. 26).

Ashton-Warner characterizes children as having two visions, an inner and an outer, and she believes the inner is more powerful and must be accessed if learning is to occur. Ashton-Warner reached this inner vision through what she calls 'key vocabulary.' These are words that have intense meaning to children and are 'already part of the dynamic life' (p. 32). Key vocabulary for the Maori children consisted of such words as 'Mummy,' 'Daddy,' 'kiss,' 'frightened,' and 'ghost,' which Ashton-Warner wrote down on cards for each child. Each student would then develop his or her own set of key words and Ashton-Warner would have the student read the cards back to her. The children also would read their words to other students in pairs; by doing this the students would quickly develop basic reading skills.

After the student had developed about forty words in the key vocabulary, Ashton-Warner moved to organic writing. She says: 'Whereas the Key Vocabulary is a one-word caption of the inner world, creative writing is a sentence-length or story-length caption' (p. 47). These sentences and stories are usually autobiographical. For Ashton-Warner writing, spelling, and composition emerge holistically. She states: 'Spelling and composition are no longer separate subjects to be taught but emerge naturally as another medium' (p. 49). Drawings are combined with the stories to form what she calls 'the most dramatic and pathetic and colourful things I've ever seen on pages' (p. 49).

The ideas for the stories always come from the students. She does not give them something to write about, which she calls an imposition:

I never teach a child something and then get him to write about it. It would be an imposition in the way that it is in art. A child's writing is his own affair and is an exercise in integration which makes for better work. The more it means to him the more value it is to him. And it means everything to him. It is part of him as an arranged subject could never be. It is not a page of sentences written round set words, resulting in a jumble of disconnected facts as you so often see. It is the unbroken line of thought that we cultivate so carefully in our own writing and conversation. (pp. 49–50)

Ashton-Warner taught math to the Maori children in the same organic way. For her, nature and number are intimately linked and many of her classes were held outdoors. She taught them about the 'Golden Section,' which is the ideal proportion in nature and is 'the division of a distance in such a way that the shorter part is to the longer part as the longer part is to the whole' (p. 68). Ashton-Warner states that fern fronds make wonderful things for young children to count. The Golden Section 'becomes inseparable from writing and reading and drawing and conversation. Three ducks on the wing we like better than three ducks on a number card with a static three beside them' (p. 70).

Ashton-Warner's approach to subject matter is to start with the inner vision of the child and build on it. The inner vision becomes the key vocabulary that in turn forms the basis for writing and reading. Her pedagogy, then, is rooted in the inner person and is connected to nature. As much as possible, she avoids artificial impositions on the child's inner vision.

Ashton-Warner (1964) quotes C.E. Beeby at the beginning of her chapter on organic writing, and it is worth citing here as a conclusion to this section because it sums up her holistic approach so well: 'Life as a whole is too complicated to teach to children. The minute it is cut up they can understand it, but you are liable to kill it in cutting it up' (p. 46).

Connections among Subjects

Connections among subjects is also referred to as integrated curriculum. This can occur at a number of levels (Figure 8.1). The first level is the *multidisciplinary*. Here the curriculum retains separate subjects but establishes linkages between them. For example, the history teacher might reference the literature and art of a specific historical period and explore how the art was representative of that period. At the *interdisciplinary* level, two or three subjects are integrated around a theme or problem. For example, in examining the problem of city traffic and other problems of urban planning, subjects such as economics, political science, design technology, and mathematics can be brought together and integrated. At the *transdisciplinary* level, several subjects are integrated around a broad theme. Issues such as poverty and violence in society lend themselves to this broadly integrative approach. At each level, connections between subjects and concepts become more numerous and complex.

Interdisciplinary Level: Holistic Thinking

At this level subjects are integrated through problems. Problem-solving approaches, such as the Wallas model described in Chapter 6, can be used. I have made some modifications in the Wallas approach to include the following steps: uncertainty/ambiguity; problem clarification; preparation/frameworking; incubation; alternative search; illumination/alternative selection; verification.

Figure 8.1 Integrated/Holistic Curriculum

Multidisciplinary	Interdisciplinary	Transdisciplinary or Holistic
Separate subjects; there may be some linkages through content	Integration of two or three subjects around problems, questions, or limited themes	Integration of nearly all subjects around broad patterns or themes

←――――――――――――――――――――――――――――――――→

Transmission	Transaction	Transformation

Uncertainty/Ambiguity

Most problem solving is prodded by an unresolved situation. For example, when I was writing this book, the lack of clarity about holistic education was a factor that encouraged me to explore this area in more depth. I had done some exploration in a course I teach entitled 'The Holistic Curriculum,' but still there was a great deal of ambiguity in my mind about both the context and practice of the holistic curriculum. In a sense, this book was a chance to explore holistic education in a more complete way.

Problem Clarification

In this step the person or group attempts to get some sort of handle on the problem. This might be done by writing out a problem statement. Unlike logical, mathematical problem solving, the problem statement is not a hypothesis in the technical sense; instead, it attempts to get at the root of the problem. Imagery and intuition can be used at this stage to help sort out the problem; by inner reflection the central issue may come forth. When I was writing this book, problem clarification involved settling on the definition of holistic education presented in

Chapter 1. This definition was one I had been working with for two years in discussions with my students, although I reworked it again for this book. The definition has provided an initial framework for the book. I have modified the definition slightly for this revised edition by using the word soul rather than self.

Preparation / Frameworking

Here one attempts to develop a more complete framework for the problem in order to see the problem from a broader perspective. For the book, this involved developing an outline in the form of chapter headings that were also congruent with the definition. This step tends to involve more linear thinking as each aspect of the framework is explored; however, imagery and intuition can still be at play here. It is possible, for example, for one to have an image of either part of the framework or a vision of the entire approach.

Incubation

Incubation can occur throughout the problem-solving process. In fact, although these steps are presented in a linear order, the approach I am describing is really much more fluid and is not a step-by-step process.

Incubation involves standing back and letting the elements work themselves through at a subconscious level. If we force the problem-solving process too much, then it will be much less productive. In working on this book as well as others I have written, I often find that ideas pop into my head while meditating, walking, driving, or taking a bath.

Alternative Search

This usually involves a more conscious search for alternatives as well as an examination of the alternatives. Alternative courses of action are first explored and developed, and then judged against criteria. These criteria can be developed consciously and can include a number of factors, or only a few which are felt more intuitively. Ultimately, these criteria are usually related to the framework. It is also possible that examining alternatives can change the original framework. Again, this whole problem-solving process tends to go back and forth rather than being a logical sequence. For example, I reworked the original definition of holistic education after I began the second half of this book.

With this book I have also attempted to link ideas for each chapter to the overall conception of holistic education. With regard to metaphor I had to consider whether this topic was congruent with the overall conception and whether it would also stimulate teacher interest. Are the examples of metaphor in the classroom adequate, I thought, or should I look for others?

Alternative Selection / Illumination

This stage involves settling on a course of action. This can entail a rational assessment of the alternatives against the criteria or it may involve the appearance of an image as outlined in Chapter 6. If an image or intuitive insight does occur, it can also be assessed against the criteria; but we have to be careful that our criteria and mindset don't become too rigid. If the criteria are too inflexible, creativity will be stifled. If the vision is a powerful one, the criteria themselves may have to be reworked.

Verification

Now the solution must be tested. In short, does it work or must you search for other solutions? With regard to this book, it must be reviewed by anonymous readers. These reviewers may recommend alternatives which can range from reworking small sections of the text, to reorganizing and rewriting a large amount of material. The reviewers are an important first step in verification of the book, and a second step in the verification comes from the type of readership the book develops.

This model can also be applied to problems and projects that the student confronts in different subjects. For example, let us examine the problem of whether a nation should be part of a larger trading bloc:

1. *Uncertainty/ambiguity.* Here the uncertainty focuses on what issues are at stake in joining a trading bloc. Issues usually focus on loss of national control (e.g., tariffs) on some industries versus possible economic gains. However, issues are not just limited to economics, as culture is often affected. Thus, students could examine possible effects on the arts as well as the economic implications.
2. *Problem clarification.* Should my country be part of a large trading bloc (e.g., NAFTA)?

3. *Preparation/frameworking.* In this step students attempt to see the underlying issues that affect the decision to be part of a large trading bloc. Some people see a conflict between two groups: business interests and environmental groups. Business and large corporations argue that free trade will enhance the economy and create more jobs. From another perspective, there is concern that large trading blocs override local interests, which include environmental concerns. Science, then, can be included in this unit to examine relevant environmental issues.

4. *Incubation.* Let the students step back from the problem for a while. They can discuss the issues involved, but it can be helpful just to let things sit (e.g., a few days) as they grapple with the issues and their vision of what interests are most important.

5. *Alternative search.* Here the students deal with the issue more consciously as they develop their vision more clearly and examine the consequences of each position. The students approach this systematically by writing out their position and listing the advantages and disadvantages of having joined a free trade bloc. Their vision becomes the criterion for assessing being part of NAFTA.

6. *Alternative selection/illumination.* The students decide whether they believe being part of a trading bloc is positive or negative. After the more systematic alternative search, the students can step back again and do some more reflection on the decision. After the inner reflection, there is a greater chance that the decision will not be an abstract one but one more connected to the whole person. The student can then write down a decision and the reasons for it.

7. *Verification.* In this last step, the students can share their answers with other students and the teacher. They can also compare it with other student responses.

In this process students looked at economics, arts, and science, although other subjects could be included as well. The Wallas model has been adapted and reworked by others. For example Roger von Oech has developed a seven-step model with two phases:

Germinal Phase

1. **Motivation** – the desire to be creative generating the energy.
2. **Search** – information gathering, looking in other fields for ideas, looking at the big picture, being willing to go astray exploring other areas.

3. **Manipulation** – transforming and manipulating the resources and ideas found, delaying judgment, and eliminating some old assumptions.
4. **Incubation** – walking away from the problem after a time of focused attention and turning it over to the subconscious. Letting go will put the problem into perspective, and the planted idea will grow in the subconscious. Delaying action will often improve ideas.
5. **Illumination** – the Aha! or Eureka experiences. Ideas can strike at any time, so always carry a means of recording an idea. Recognise your creative time of the day. Don't overwork, and put aside time for Re-Creation.

Practical Phase

6. **Evaluation** – making a decision even if the ideas aren't perfect.
7. **Action** – completing the Creative Process can be the most difficult step of all.

The focus of the creativity techniques is on the Germinal Phase and how we can generate and manipulate ideas. (van Oech, n.d.)

Teachers can choose from a variety of problem-solving processes that can allow for subject connections. By employing these models in different disciplines we can explore connections between the subjects. My purpose in presenting the above approach is to explore approaches to problem solving that are less linear and allow for intuition, incubation, and imagery.

Transdisciplinary Model:
Waldorf Education/Main Lesson

In the Waldorf school the morning's instruction begins with the main lesson, which runs from approximately 9:00 to 11:00 A.M. In Waldorf education the same teacher stays with the children from grades 1 to 8, and one of their main responsibilities each day is the main lesson.

The main lesson brings together English, mathematics, geography, history, and science. The main vehicle for integration is the artistic sense of the teacher. The lesson can often start with singing or a speech chorus of poems that the students are learning. Steiner recognized that young children love ritual, and it is built into many aspects of the program. The singing might be followed by teacher presentation on the main theme.

Central to each main lesson are the arts, as it is the artistic sense that integrates the main lesson. Each student has an unlined notebook in which they draw in colour what they are learning. According to Richards (1980):

Each Main Lesson will call upon the child's powers of listening, of body movement, of thinking, and of feeling. Artistic activity is particularly related to the will: it is an experience of doing, of making. Artwork also invites the child's feeling for expressiveness and encourages a kind of intuitive thinking about how to get things done. In the early grades, some teachers allow the children to copy what has been drawn on the board so that they may learn to draw in ways they would not otherwise know. Other times the children draw freely. Variety exists, according to teacher and grade. (p. 25)

Wax crayons, coloured pencils, and watercolours are used. The student is encouraged to feel the colour as he or she draws so that the artistic experience is not abstract. In the early grades the colouring can follow the telling of a story so that language is connected to art. The student may mix primary colours such as yellow and blue to make green. Again a story is often told before the mixing of the colours so the experience is connected to the child's imagination. Black and white are not usually mixed at the lower grades because they are more abstract and not as dynamic for the younger child. Similarly, the children do not draw outline shapes but fill in shapes with colour. Shapes tend to come from the colour rather than from hard boundaries. Art is also connected to math as painting, modelling, designing, and string constructions are used (Richards, 1980).

Storytelling can be used in teaching science. For example, Wilkinson (1975) suggests that the following story is helpful for teaching young children about the four elements:

Once upon a time there was a big brown seed, with white edges and white stripes, which was lying on the ground. The gnomes who lived in that part of the garden knew that it was a seed and that they ought to look after it, so they quietly buried it. Then they told the water fairies about it and the water fairies came down in the rain to give it something to drink. Soon the fire fairies who live in the sun's warmth came on a visit and the seed began to feel strange, as if some change were taking place. It seemed to be getting bigger and soon its jacket burst. One shoot went downwards into the earth and another shoot came up out of the ground. The little shoot that went downwards grew into a root and all the springtime the gnomes were busy looking after it and the soil around it. The rain and the fire fairies kept visiting the growing plant, and the air fairies also came and danced around it. For months it grew, taller than you, and as tall as I am, and then, at the top of the stalk something quite wonderful happened. A huge yellow flower appeared turning its face towards the sun. Some children came to look at it and they said, 'What a big shining face, just like the sun. We will call it a sunflower.' (p. 72)

In grade 5, one teacher made the following connection between botany, music, and poetry:

As an introduction to our study of the plant kingdom, I led the children from a dramatic story of the seed's awakening to their own creative expressions of this birth of life forces. Each child discovered a tonal harmony which we then moved to by using our cupped hands to be the seed. Then as the melody was played, our hands followed the opening of the seed, roots' first search, uplifting of the seed-enclosed seed leaves, breaking into light and warmth, spreading of the seed leaves, upward striving of the stem and then the first true leaves. All this formed by a few notes! A poem-like expression followed. (Richards, 1980, p. 114)

The students wrote a tune, which they then played on the recorder, and then wrote a poem. Richards (1980) argues that through art Waldorf education attempts to develop an intuitive seeing that is missing in our culture:

It is an intuitive seeing, which comes about as a result of exercising and experiencing one's physical senses imaginatively, wholeheartedly, and wholesoulfully. This is why artistic practice is so important in all learning and education. This is why neglect of the artist in each person is so impoverishing to society. Without this spiritual sense organ, this way of seeing the formative forces at work in a physical process, we are blind and duped by appearances. (p. 73)

Steiner encouraged teachers to be creative and flexible in their approach. According to Richards (1980), they 'paint and draw, sing and play recorder, recite and tell stories, and cook and play with the children' (p. 28). Steiner wanted the teacher to appeal to the interests of the child and to also use humour and surprise in the classroom. He wanted the teachers to teach from enthusiasm rather than a rigid schedule. Steiner (1976) said to teachers at the first Waldorf school before it opened:

> The teacher must be a person of initiative in everything that he does, great and small ...
>
> The teacher should be one who is interested in the being of the whole world and of humanity ...
>
> The teacher must be one who never makes a compromise in his heart and mind with what is untrue ...
>
> The teacher must never get stale or grow sour ...
>
> During this fortnight I have only spoken of what can enter directly into your practical teaching, if you allow it first to work rightly within your own souls. But our Waldorf School, my dear friends, will depend upon what you do within yourselves, and whether you really allow the things which we have been considering to become effective in your own souls ...
>
> I do not want to make you into teaching machines, but into free independent teachers ...
>
> Let us in particular keep before us this thought which shall truly fill our hearts and minds: That bound up with the spiritual movement of the present day are also the spiritual powers that guide the Universe. If we believe in these good spiritual powers, then they will be the inspirers of our lives and we shall really be enabled to teach. (pp. 199–201)

James Beane

James Beane (1997) is an advocate of interdisciplinary integrated curriculum. Beane believes that the curriculum should move away from fragmented approaches where knowledge is kept within the boundaries of separate subjects. For Beane, the central features of integrated curriculum include:

> First, the curriculum is organized around problems and issues that are of personal and social significance in the real world. Second, learning experiences in relation to the organizing center are planned so as to integrate pertinent knowledge in the context of the organizing centers. Third, knowledge is developed and used to address the organizing center currently under study rather than to prepare for some later test or grade level. Finally, emphasis is placed on substantive projects and other activities that involve real application of knowledge. (p. 9)

The final key feature of Beane's approach is the participation of students in curriculum planning. He suggests that students participate by identifying questions related to personal issues and those that are oriented towards society and culture. The former could include questions such as 'What kind of job will I have when I become an adult?' and 'Will I get married?' Society-oriented questions might include 'Why do people hate each other?' and 'Will racism ever end?' After all the questions have been put up on the board or chart paper, the teacher negotiates with the students themes, or organizing centres, based on the questions. These themes are usually broad and include 'conflict and violence,' 'living in the future,' and 'money.' Beane suggests using a concept web with the central theme in the middle and a number of sub-themes surrounding the main theme. The students research the theme and sub-themes and then can present their conclusions through some kind of activity or performance. For example, a class focusing on the environment decided to divided into five sub-groups to create five large-scale biomes in their classroom. Another class working with the theme of living in the future developed a vision of what their city will be like in the year 2030.

The Story Model

This transdisciplinary model of integrated curriculum and learning was developed by Susan Drake and her associates (Drake, 1998; Drake et al., 1992). It focuses on global, cultural, and personal change and uses the concept of story as the frame. It includes the following assumptions:

- The world as we know it is undergoing flux and change.
- We make meaning through story.
- Knowledge is interconnected.
- Knowledge is laden with cultural values, beliefs and assumptions.
- Most of these values, beliefs and assumptions are held at an unconscious level.
- Our actions are driven by these beliefs.
- To change actions, we have to become conscious of our cultural values, beliefs and assumptions.
- We can consciously create a 'new story' to live by. (Drake, 1998, p. 100)

The model acknowledges that there are different levels of stories, including personal, cultural, and global. The personal story is how we make meaning of our own lives. The cultural story focuses on the history of the culture or subcultures in which we live. Again, it is important to acknowledge that there is not one cultural story, but several versions of the story depending on the framework of the storyteller. Finally, there is the global story, which connects personal and cultural stories and places them in an even larger context. Figure 8.2 is a diagram of the story model.

The student can start by identifying the present story. Often this story focuses on a large theme such as family, education, or the economy. Students identify what they see as the main elements of the present story. For example, if the students are focusing on education, the story can concentrate on such issues as the concern for greater accountability, the inclusive school, and school reform and restructuring. From the present story the students look at the past story of education, which has often been a conflict between traditional and progressive forces in education.

Predominant, however, has been transmission learning, in which information has been transmitted to students for feedback on tests. Students list the characteristics of the past and present stories. After examining the past and present stories, the students are ready to look at a new story. They develop a new story by creating an ideal story and

Figure 8.2 The Story Model

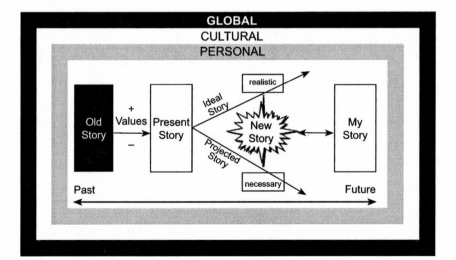

a projected story. The ideal is a vision of what they would like to see happen, although it is tempered by realism. For example, this might include a vision of holistic education. However, they also develop a vision of opposing trends that are part of the present story. For example, the concern for accountability could lead to a test-driven curriculum that is too rigid to account for individual or group differences. After developing the ideal story and the projected story, the students start to shape a new story which is a synthesis of the two. From the new story, they also attempt to formulate their own actions and individual story in relation to the new story. Thus, the new story could be some sort of balance between accountability and a more global, holistic approach to education.

After this initial overview, students can develop a set of inquiry questions around the relevant issue (e.g., education). These should be open-ended questions that allow for reflection and deliberation. After developing the questions, the students do research on each question. Students can work in groups, and once they have focused on the questions, they can develop some sort of presentation or exhibition around the issue and the questions that they have focused on. For more details on this approach, see Drake et al. (1992).

Subject and Community

Subjects can also provide a bridge to the community. For example, students can use the community as a resource to collect and write stories about former students and teachers from their schools. They can interview former teachers and students and then put together a book of stories to create an oral history of the school. Student artists can draw pictures or take photographs of the participants. This not only provides a bridge to the community; it also helps to build a school mythology (Miller, 2000).

Owen Valley High School in Spencer, Indiana, uses a holistic approach to integrating its academic and vocational curricula. Students write stories on local history that involve a collaboration of classes in creative writing, civics, child development, English, computer applications, Spanish, drama, and math. The stories are then published in book form (Kinzer, 1997).

Environmental education can provide a vehicle for connecting a school subject to the surrounding community. Chapter 10 gives an example of how a principal in Japan used the project of planting a small forest on school property to connect a school activity to the surrounding community.

Confluent Education

I would like to close this chapter with a brief discussion of confluent education, which has developed a number of strategies to facilitate connections between self and subject, subject and subject, and subject and community. Confluent education began in the 1960s under the leadership of George Brown and initially focused on connecting the cognitive and affective domains. Confluent education was an important forerunner of holistic education.

Below are some examples of confluent education exploring the various subject connections.

Self and Subject

The following example by Jean Schleifer (1975) focuses on how students can make connections with a novel they have been reading, particularly with a character who was important to the student:

1. Close your eyes. Get into your own private space. Now from the book you read, try to see the person who means the most to you. Put the person somewhere, either in a place he would naturally be according to the book or a place where you can imagine his being. Try to see every part of the person. What does the hair look like? What color? Length? Curly? Straight? Windblown? Neat? Notice the ears. What kind of nose? Notice the skin. Clear, pimply, tanned? How do you see the mouth? Full? Drooped? Clenched? What is the person doing with the hands? How does the person stand? Walk? What kind of clothes? See them distinctly – the colors, the style, etc.
2. When you are ready, open your eyes. Write a description of your person's appearance.
3. Choose one word from what you have written that is the essence of the description of the person. Write it down.
4. Now write down what to you would be an opposite word – one word.
5. Tell your words. Talk about them.
6. Turn your paper over. Draw, in lines or colors, the way you see the person. Don't try to draw a photographic picture. Show the person through shapes, colors, and lines. Talk to others. (p. 252)

This exercise also asks the student to use art (drawing), so it also makes a subject–subject connection.

Subject and Subject

The following activity is from Gloria Castillo's *Left-handed Teaching: Lessons in Affective Education* (1978) and makes connections between science, language, drama, and movement.

Lesson 14. Solar System Conversations

Be the sun. Talk as if you are the sun. Example: 'I am the sun. I am a very large star. I have a great deal of heat. My heat gives energy to the earth.'

Now, be the earth. Talk as if you are the earth. Example: 'I am the earth. I have air, water, plants, and animals.'

One person be the sun and another be the earth. Create a conversation between the sun and the earth. What do you have to say to one another?

Let this be an activity in improvisational theater as well as in science. Do not correct the students if they should offer incorrect statements. After the 'play,' you can clarify points, give additional information, or assign further readings. Use this activity to assess what the students do and do not know about the sun and the earth.

With advanced students, add other planets of our solar system to the 'play.'

Dance around as if you are the earth. Circle the room once to represent one day. Choose a partner. One be the earth, the other the moon. Earth and moon dance together, in time to one another. Now both join another partnership. Two of you become the sun. All of you dance together as if you are the sun (two students), moon, and earth dancing together.

Depending on the ability of the class to do this, continue to add students to represent other solar bodies. Create a solar system dance. (pp. 194–5)

Subject and Community

Sandra Newby (1975) developed a program for her grade 9 English class that included a community component. She encouraged her students to organize a newspaper, record interviews, and produce video-tapes based on contact with someone outside the school.

References

Ashton-Warner, S. (1964). *Teacher*. New York: Bantam.

Beane, J. (1997). *Curriculum integration: Designing the core of democratic education*. New York: Teachers College Press.

Brown, G.I., Phillips, M., & Shapiro, S. (1976). *Getting it all together: Confluent education*. Bloomington, IN: Phi Delta Kappa Educational Foundation.

Castillo, G. (1978). *Left-handed teaching: Lessons in affective education*. New York: Holt Rinehart and Winston.

Drake, S.M. (1998). *Creating integrated curriculum: Proven ways to increase student learning*. Thousand Oaks, CA: Corwin.

Drake, S. M., Bebbington, J., Laksman, S., Mackie, P., Maynes, N., & Wayne, L. (1992). *Developing an integrated curriculum using the story model*. Toronto: OISE Press.

Kinzer, T. (1997). Spinning a yarn. *Techniques: Making education and career connections, 72*(8), 18–20.

Miller, J. (2000). *Education and the soul: Toward a spiritual curriculum*. Albany, NY: SUNY Press.

Newby, S. (1975). Getting at responsibility in a ninth-grade English class. In G.I. Brown (Ed.), *The live classroom: Innovation through confluent education and gestalt* (pp. 198–205). New York: Viking.

Richards, M.V. (1980). *Toward wholeness: Rudolf Steiner education in America*. Middletown, CT: Wesleyan University Press.

Schleifer, J. (1975). Listening to the book. In G.E. Brown (Ed.), *The live classroom: Innovation through confluent education and gestalt* (pp. 252–4). New York: Viking.

Steiner, R. (1976). *Practical advice for teachers*. London: Rudolf Steiner Press.

von Oech, R. (n.d). *A Whack, a Kick and a Poke* cassette program. http:members.optusnet.com.au/-charles57/Creative/Brain/vonoech.htm

Wilkinson, R. (1975). *Common sense schooling*. Hastings, Sussex: Henry Goulden.

CHAPTER NINE

Community Connections

The holistic curriculum should foster connections between student and community. The most immediate community for the student is the classroom. Cooperative education, with its emphasis on learning teams, attempts to foster community within classrooms. Ideally the school as a whole should be a community, or a sanctuary, in Secretan's (1996) terms. It is also important for the school to extend itself into the surrounding community, and there are programs which involve the student in community service activities or in social change programs. Finally global education attempts to connect the student to the global community. This chapter offers some suggestions for creating community within the whole school.

Building Community in Classrooms

One of the key factors to creating community in the classroom is to provide a psychologically safe environment. In the last chapter I discuss some of the skills that are important to this process. Perhaps the most important factor is simply being present and mindful to students (see Chapter 12).

One helpful teaching/learning strategy is cooperative learning. Cooperative learning employs small groups in which students learn to trust each other and work together. Roger and David Johnson (1994) suggest that cooperative learning encourages students to feel responsible for others' learning as well as their own. For example, in a spelling lesson students work in small groups to help each other learn the words. For the Johnsons, cooperative learning includes the following elements.

1. clearly perceived positive interdependence
2. considerable promotive (face-to-face) interaction
3. clearly perceived individual accountability and personal responsibility to achieve the group's goals
4. frequent use of the relevant interpersonal and small group skills
5. frequent and regular processing of current functioning to improve the group's future effectiveness (p. 2)

Positive interdependence refers to students working together. This means that students not only learn the material or skills themselves but ensure that all members of the group learn the material as well. The element of positive interdependence is related to the concept of interconnectedness, which is fundamental to integrative teaching and holistic learning. The Johnsons suggest that this interdependence can be facilitated in a number of ways. One method is through positive goal interdependence, in which students focus on a common goal. Another way is through positive rewards that celebrate interdependence; for example, the group might receive bonus points if everyone meets the basic criteria on a test or assignment. A third way to foster interdependence is by encouraging the group members to share resources. Finally, interdependence can be facilitated through assigning group members various roles. Glasser (1986) identifies four roles for group members:

1. Encourager of participation. In a friendly way encourages all members of the group to participate in the discussion, sharing their ideas and feelings.
2. Praiser. Compliments group members who do their assigned work and contribute to the learning of the group.
3. Summarizer. Restates the ideas and feelings expressed in the discussion whenever it is appropriate.
4. Checker. Makes sure everyone has read and edited two compositions and that everyone understands the general principles of writing thesis essays. (p. 100)

Face-to-face promotive interaction is an essential element in cooperative learning as the students work together by encouraging each other, sharing ideas and resources, providing feedback to each other, challenging each other's conclusion or assumptions to help reach the best decisions, and demonstrating care for the other members.

Individual accountability means that one or two members should not carry the group and let the others coast. Individual accountability can be facilitated by keeping the size of the group small, randomly calling on one of the group members to report on how the group is doing, observing group behaviour and individual participation in the group, and assigning one member the role of checker.

Interpersonal and small-group skills is the fourth element in cooperative learning. It is important that the students learn to communicate and listen effectively, resolve conflicts when they arise, and generally be able to support one another and the group process.

Group processing is the final component of cooperative learning. This element focuses on how well the group has been working together. This can occur during the group task, in which members step back and ask how they are doing as a group, and at the end, when a summative evaluation is required. Group members can simply ask what has been working well and where they need to improve. Teachers can also give the group feedback on what they have observed.

The Johnsons refer to over 875 studies that have demonstrated the positive effects of cooperative learning on student growth and achievement. Cooperative learning has also facilitated higher-level reasoning, more frequent generation of new ideas, and greater transfer of learning from one situation to another.

Circles of Learning

Another vehicle for creating community is to have the students form an entire circle. The circle has its roots in indigenous cultures; for example, some First Nations people form a circle and pass the talking stick around to give each person a chance to share their thoughts and feelings. Black Elk said this about circles:

> Everything the Power of the World does is done in a circle.
> The sky is round, and I have heard that the earth is round like a ball, and so are all the stars. The wind, in its greatest power, whirls. Birds make their nests in circles, for theirs is the same religion as ours ... The life of a (person) is a circle from childhood to childhood, and it is in everything where power moves. (as cited in Baldwin, 1994, p. 80)

The talking stick can be used in the classroom as well, giving each student a chance to speak. The circle can focus on a specific topic or have an open agenda.

A circle that focuses on problem solving (Glasser, 1969) can follow a specific step-by-step process. Glasser suggests six steps: (1) creating a climate of involvement, (2) exposing the problem, (3) making a personal value judgment, (4) identifying alternative courses of action, (5) making a commitment, and (6) behavioural follow-up.

I use the circle in all my classes more as a vehicle for sharing stories than for problem solving. I find it an exceptionally powerful way to share important student experiences in the classroom. For example, in my spirituality in education class I ask students to share a soulful experience from their own life. As we go around I am always moved by the students' stories, which include experiences in nature, illness of a family member, and experiences with the arts.

Baldwin (1994) believes that the circle can be an agent of societal transformation. She describes a process for adults to participate in what she calls the PeerSpirit Circle. She makes reference to the work of Jeanne Gibbs (1987), who has developed the concept of tribes for use in classrooms. The tribe is a small classroom group of five or six children who work together throughout the school year. Gibbs also uses the large classroom circle to allow students to share events in their lives. Baldwin summarizes the work of Gibbs this way:

Students in tribes have their contributions and feelings acknowledged throughout the process: they feel safe, they feel loyal, they feel loved and loving. In thousands of classrooms, the tribal community is preparing children to become adult citizens of the circle. (p. 159)

School Community

Ideally, the school itself should be a community where students feel they belong. Secretan (1996) has identified three types of organizations. One is the mechanistic school, where roles are strictly defined and people do not feel fully accepted. The second is the chaotic organization, where people have more individual freedom. Third is the sanctuary, where people feel affirmed. For Secretan, the sanctuary is 'not a collection of parts but an integrated system of souls – not so much a place but a state of mind in which they may flourish' (p. 38). In the sanctuary, people's feelings and thoughts are acknowledged. Both teachers and students look forward to being at school, as they feel that their souls are nourished by the environment they find there. This environment is one of respect, caring, and even reverence. People feel validated as human beings and can speak authentically from their hearts. Love predominates rather than fear. Most of all, there is a deep sense of community. In fact, in the sanctuary, people do not just communicate or exchange ideas, they experience communion with one another. Communion is where soul touches soul.

The sanctuary, like the chaotic organization, also includes spontaneity and fun. It nurtures creativity and holistic learning that integrates body, mind, emotions, and spirit.

There are no recipes for developing a sanctuary or a soulful school. However, we can begin to create conditions that allow for the development of soul. Some of the things that a school staff can do are:

1. *Recognize the importance of the non-verbal.* When we focus on the non-verbal, or that silent space, we become aware of how we carry ourselves, how we engage others through eye contact and the tone of our voice. We realize that the quality of our being and presence has as much impact on student development as anything we say. When we become aware of the non-verbal, then a balance can develop between talk and silence. At all levels, education has focused on verbal exchange. We have forgotten about the rest of our bodies and how we can communicate in silence. A warm smile directed to a child can send a message of support and love.

2. *Pay attention to the aesthetic environment of the school and classroom.* We can help transform schools into sanctuaries by making the physical environment more beautiful. For example, plants can become part of the school decor in the halls and in the classrooms. Walls can be painted in soft, warm colours. Artwork, both student artwork and professional artwork, can be placed on the walls. However, there needs to be a balance. Sometimes classroom walls are completely covered so that we cannot really notice what is there. So don't overdo it, and leave plenty of space around the art that is put up. In the Waldorf classrooms for the younger children, there are sometimes pictures of the Madonna and child: it is felt that the warmth of this picture can have a healing effect on the children. As much as possible, we can soften the school environment. Some classrooms have couches where students can sit and read.

3. *Tell stories about the school.* Every school has a story or, more accurately, a set of stories. Teachers and students can collect these stories and put them together in a booklet or recite them on special school occasions. If stories are shared teachers and students can begin to see the continuity and uniqueness of their school over time. The pro-

cess of collecting stories can be helpful as students interview former students or members of the surrounding community. Sketches
(both written and visual) can be constructed of former teachers and
students. The set of stories can eventually create a mythology for
the school. This mythology contains a shared sense of meaning and
values for the school. Telling stories about the school can allow re-
curring themes to emerge that can form the heart of the school's
mythology. For example, do the stories tend to focus on academic
achievement, sports, or community service, or some combination of
the three? Private schools often engage in this practice of telling stories and creating a shared sense of meaning, but I see no reason why
this cannot also happen in the public schools, which also have their
own unique histories.

4. *Have celebrations and rituals.* Rituals help give people a sense of connection to their communities. The most common ritual and celebration in schools is graduation. However, there is no reason to limit
rituals and celebrations to this one event. Celebrations could be conducted to mark changes in the seasons. These celebrations could include playing music, reading poetry, and telling stories. Rituals can
be part of the daily life of the school, and the use of the circle in the
classroom discussed above can also become a ritual.

5. *Value truth and authenticity.* Secretan argues that telling the truth is
an important aspect of cultivating soul in the workplace. When we
live in an atmosphere where people do not tell the truth, integrity
and community break down. As much as possible, leaders should
attempt to speak and live according to what they see as truth. We
should recognize that we are imperfect human beings but also that
our integrity comes from our ability to live authentic lives. One of
the behaviours that helps build authenticity is promise-keeping.
When we keep our promises, others can learn to depend on our
word. Sometimes in schools, gaps can develop between what we
say and what we do. For example, a principal might talk about the
importance of collegial decision making and then make all the important decisions on her own. When a gap develops between what a
principal says and does, cynicism develops. Trust is almost non-ex-
istent. On the other hand, when we work with someone who we feel
is trustworthy and authentic we can feel empowered and willing to
take risks and be creative.

6. *Encourage a nourishing voice.* A soulful school is a place where people
can speak without fear. According to David Whyte (1994):

Inhabiting the full body, the long body, as many North American Native traditions say, with the voice, may be one of the great soul challenges of adult life. If the voice originates and ends its journey in the bodies of the speaker and listener, it is also true that many parts of our bodies are struck deaf or dumb from an early age. We walk through the door into the organization every morning looking like full-grown adults but many parts of us are still playing emotional catch-up. (p. 127)

Whyte suggests that one of the ways we can reclaim our voice is to learn to say no. By saying no we gradually learn to say yes to what we ultimately value and feel is important to our soul. Of course, the leaders in our schools must be comfortable cultivating an environment where voice can be heard. The principal needs to be aware, of course, of her own voice. Each of us needs to ask ourselves: where I am speaking from? Am I speaking mostly from my head or from the deeper part of myself?

Social Literacy Training

Alfred Alschuler (1980) has developed an approach to developing school community based on the work of Paulo Freire (1972). Freire's work has been an inspiration to many social-oriented educators who desire major reforms in both school and society. Alschuler has used Freire's model to develop a practical approach to developing a sense of community within schools. Social literacy training develops social skills in students and helps build community in classrooms and schools.

Alschuler claims that Freire's philosophy consists of three major principles. The first involves creating 'a world in which it is easier to love' (1972, p. 24). Freire focuses on oppressive social and economic conditions that make it difficult for people to realize their potential as human beings. Oppression is a situation in which one group gets a disproportionate reward for what they contribute. For example, it is oppressive when landowners hire workers at low wages while they reap huge profits. Alschuler also feels school can be oppressive when educators control all the resources (e.g., grades and rewards) and do not allow the students to have any say over their own learning. This type of environment makes it difficult for teachers and students to interact in an open, caring way.

The second principle is developing the ability of people to create their own world. Freire argues that people learn to create a world in which it is easier to love in three stages. In the first stage, the *magical-conforming*, people do not recognize the oppression and are passive. At this stage teachers tend to say, 'Kids will always act that way,' and, because of this belief, will make few efforts to encourage positive student growth. In the second stage, the *naive-reforming*, people believe that all difficulties lie with the individual and do not look at system rules and norms. A teacher at this stage will blame himself for problems he is having rather than connecting his behaviour to the surrounding context. Although some problems can be solved at the individual level, more serious difficulties may be related to school procedures and norms. In the third stage, the *critical-transforming*, people realize that they must critique the institutions that govern their lives and collaborate to change those institutions. At this stage teachers work to identify and solve problems. Teachers do not work in isolation, which can happen so often in schools, but work together to improve their instructional and classroom management strategies.

The third principle of Freire's social literacy training is developing problem-solving strategies to deal with conflict and oppression. At the heart of problem-solving strategies are three processes. First, the teachers or students name the important conflicts. This can involve generating a list of key words that characterize the conflict or problem. Second, the teachers or students analyse the system causes of conflict. The problem solvers try to get behind the difficulty to examine the norms and systematic nature of the conflict. In the third step, the problem solvers engage in collaborative action to deal with the difficulty.

Social literacy training involves a variety of strategies to create community within schools. Sometimes these strategies can involve teachers meeting together in small groups to deal with problems. Listed below are some of the solutions developed by social literacy groups:

- One group wanted to reduce referrals to the office. Instead of sending students to the vice-principal, the teachers in one social literacy group made a 'mutual aid agreement': disruptive incidents were defused by sending the student to another teacher's class or having one of the teachers in the social literacy group come into another teacher's class to help deal with the problem. Office referrals in this school were reduced by 75 per cent.
- Three teachers in one social literacy group identified the teaching of geography as a problem. They were then able to meet regularly to develop more relevant curriculum in this subject area.

- Some teachers were concerned about new legislation that meant special education students were to be 'mainstreamed' into regular classrooms. This social literacy group worked with special education teachers to develop an in-service program for the regular classroom teacher. During this process, they focused on developing new methods for individualizing instruction.
- In one junior high school the students moved from class to class as one group. The social literacy group in that school felt that the scheduling tended to limit student options and fix them into a narrow social role. The teachers approached a university professor to help them install flexible scheduling with the assistance of a computer.
- A social literacy group identified the use of the intercom as a problem in the school. Its use was leading to long disruptions in the classroom. The teachers met with the principal, who agreed to limit the use of the intercom.
- Teachers set up a 'care' room in the school. Teachers who participated in this project were entitled to send students to the room, where a teacher was available for special help. The room also provided a cooling-down period for students.
- Women in one school formed a consciousness-raising group to deal with the problem of sexism in the school.

Alschuler (1980) comments on these examples:

> These examples illustrate several unique characteristics of socially literate methods of reducing the discipline problem: (1) Socially Literate solutions do not blame individuals. Individuals cooperate to change the rules and roles of the system. (2) Social Literacy leads to multileveled solutions that win peace in interpersonal, classroom, and schoolwide war games. (3) Socially Literate solutions yield a broad range of outcomes related to better discipline – fewer classroom conflicts, more learning of the subject matter discipline, greater discipleship and increased personal discipline. (p. 42)

In order to facilitate problem solving, Freire (1972) encourages the use of dialogue, which is facilitated by six conditions (also cited in Alschuler 1980):

1. *Love.* 'Dialogue cannot exist ... in the absence of a profound love for the world and for human beings.'
2. *Humility*. 'Dialogue cannot exist without humility ... Dialogue, as the

encounter of human beings addressed to the common task of learning and acting, is broken if the parties (or one of them) lack humility. How can I dialogue if I always project ignorance onto others and never perceive my own? At the point of encounter ... there are only people who are attempting, together, to learn more than they now know.'

3. *Faith.* 'Dialogue ... requires an intense faith in people, faith in the power to make and re-make, to create and re-create, faith in their vocation to be more fully human.'

4. *Trust.* 'Founding itself on love, humility and faith, dialogue becomes a horizontal relationship of which mutual trust between the dialoguers is the logical consequence.'

5. *Hope.* 'As the encounter of people seeking to be more fully human, dialogue cannot be carried on in a climate of hopelessness. If the dialoguers expect nothing to come of their effort, their encounter will be empty and sterile, bureaucratic and tedious.'

6. *Critical thinking.* 'Finally, true dialogue cannot exist unless the dialoguers engage in critical thinking ... For the naive thinker, the important thing is accommodation to this normalized 'today.' For the critic, the important thing is the continuing transformation of reality on behalf of the continuing humanization of people.' (pp. 78–81)

These conditions are necessary for dialogue and are also fundamental to creating a caring school community. Dialogue also involves speaking what Freire calls 'true words.' True words are similar to Ashton-Warner's key vocabulary in that they are rooted in the lives of the students and are often related to problems they are confronting. It is very important that teachers not engage in pseudo-dialogue such as asking questions to which they already know the answer or that seem to promote intellectual posturing rather than collaborative problem solving.

Alschuler (1980) gives examples of different teachers who allow students to participate in decision making. One teacher, who taught a reading class at the junior high level, had a class that was extremely bored, so he discussed with the students ways in which the class could be improved. As a result of the discussion, part of the class time was devoted to free reading, in which students could choose the books they wanted to read while the remaining time was devoted to working on specific reading skills. After devoting time to free reading, the teacher found that the 'students have worked harder and more conscientiously on the work and have accomplished more in the way of mastery than when almost 100 percent of the time was supposedly allotted to learning skills, almost none to free reading ... Grades are up and so are attitudes and relationships' (p. 153).

Student–Community Connections

Service Learning

Service learning involves students in community activity that is also linked to academic work in the school. I would like to cite a couple of examples of service learning from two of my friends and colleagues, John Donnelly and Lourdes Arguelles.

Engaged service is the term that John Donnelly uses to describe the work he does with at-risk adolescents. The goal of this work is to develop compassion in students or the ability to see that another person's suffering is not separate from themselves. The teachings of Ram Dass have had a strong impact on John, who quotes Dass's definition of compassion:

> Compassion in action is paradoxical and mysterious. It is absolute, yet continually changing. It accepts that everything is happening exactly as it should, and it works with a full-hearted commitment to change. It sets goals but knows that the process is all there is. It is joyful in the midst of suffering and hopeful in the face of overwhelming odds. It is simple in a world of complexity and confusion. It is done for others but nurtures the self. (as cited in Donnelly, 2002, pp. 3–5)

Engaged service, then, is a process of attempting to heal this suffering in others and ourselves. John likes to use nature trips to engage his students. Yet these are not just trips to see and observe nature; they also involve students helping one another. John describes one of the activities that his students engaged in:

> On one occasion during field trip, ten of my students helped one student who was confined to a wheelchair gain mobility around a mountain camp that had not been adapted for children with specific physical needs. They assisted him off the bus, folded his wheelchair, set out his silverware at the table, and by splitting into three different teams, helped him hike on trails that were inaccessible to children with special needs. They finished a full day of these activities by helping him get ready and go to bed ... I doubt if any more love or concern could be shown by a group of students. (p. 310)

Many of the students in this program come from extremely challenging backgrounds. Yet John with this love and commitment has been
able to bring hope to many of his students. He remains hopeful that we
can offer an education that is truly life-affirming. He writes: 'Look to
the children and they will show us the way. Ask them what they need;
do not explain to them what they want. Ask them how they can help,
do not tell them what is required. Make the subject of the day a life that
can be enhanced. (p. 314)

Community-Based Work

Lourdes Arguelles teaches at Claremont Graduate School in California.
Her students range in age from mid-twenties to mid-fifties. As part of
the curriculum she has them go into grassroots communities, which are
often marginalized, either economically or socially. First, she asks her
students to spend time with people in these communities in informal
situations such as 'sharing meals and casual conversation, and doing
manual labor' (2002, p. 294). Second she encourages 'slow, non-deliber-
ate, non-formal and sporadic ways of knowing,' which she calls 'slow
mind' (p. 296). For some students the shift to slow mind was a challenge:

> When I first met my teacher I was not as ready for sustained and formal
> interaction with her as I am now. My mind was too accelerated. The time
> I have taken just talking and being with people at a low-income hous-
> ing project sort of settled me in, and I formed a bond with the other stu-
> dents and with the teacher in addition to the bonds with the people in the
> community. I also began to realize how some of the things that I do in
> my classroom and in my life can impact negatively on the lives of these
> people. That has made a real difference in my life and in my teaching. (p.
> 295)

Lourdes offers a course that challenges her students in many different ways. Through these challenges they find a way to connect more
deeply with themselves and with others.

The Global Community

Global education helps students see themselves as part of the global
community. Global education shares the same principles as holis-

tic education, particularly with regard to the concept of interdependence. David Selby (2001) argues that holistic and global education are founded on the principle of radical interconnectedness, where everything is in constant change. He refers to David Bohm's (1983) concept of holomovement as a way of looking at life and the world in terms of processes rather than as static things or selves. Selby believes that a connection between holistic education and global education is the need to recognize the importance of the inner journey and that this journey is closely linked to the outside world. He argues that the global/holistic curriculum should include the following strategies:

- cooperative, interactive learning
- children (not child) centered
- mixed-paced learning
- empathetic, embodied learning
- spiritual learning
- slow learning (p. 14)

Another important global educator is Robert Muller, who developed the concept of the World Core Curriculum (www.unol.org/rms/wcc. html). This curriculum has four main components:

1. our planetary home and our place in the universe
2. our place in time
3. the family of humanity
4. the miracle of individual life

Several schools have implemented Muller's curriculum. The first one was established in 1979 in Arlington, Texas, and functions now also as the centre for World Core Curriculum work.

Conclusion

Clearly there are many levels of community; however, it is vital that students feel a sense of community in their classroom. If this is lacking, students will not experience community on a day-to-day basis. When students experience community in their classrooms, they form connections with the other students, the teacher, and the learning process.

References

Alschuler, A. (1980). *School discipline: A socially literate solution.* New York: Mc-Graw Hill.

Arguelles, L. (2002). How we live, learn and die: How a teacher and some of her students meditated and walked on an engaged Buddhist path. In J.P. Miller and Y. Nakagawa (Eds.), *Nurturing our wholeness: Perspectives on spirituality in education* (pp.285–303). Brandon, VT: Foundation for Educational Renewal.

Baldwin, C. (1994). *Calling the circle: The first and future culture.* Newberg, OR: Swan and Raven.

Bohm, D. (1983). *Wholeness and the implicate order.* New York: Ark.

Donnelly, J. (2002). Educating for a deeper sense of self. In J.P. Miller and Y. Nakagawa (Eds.), *Nurturing our wholeness: Perspectives on spirituality in education* (pp.304–17). Brandon, VT: Foundation for Educational Renewal.

Freire, P. (1972). *Pedagogy of the oppressed.* New York: Harper & Row.

Gibbs, J. (1987). *Tribes: A process for social development and cooperative learning.* Santa Rosa, CA: Center Source Publications.

Glasser, W. (1969). *Schools without failure.* New York: Harper and Row.

Glasser, W. (1986). *Control theory in the classroom.* New York: Harper and Row.

Johnson, R.T., & Johnson, D.W. (1994). An overview of cooperative learning. In J. Thousand, A. Villa, & A. Nevin (Eds.), *Creativity and collaborative learning* (pp.1–23). Baltimore: Brookes Press.

Secretan, L.H. (1996). *Reclaiming higher ground: Creating a organizations that inspire soul.* Toronto: MacMillan.

Selby, D. (2001). The signature of the whole: Radical interconnectedness and its implications for global and environmental education. *Encounter, 14,* 5–16.

Whyte, D. (1994). *The heart aroused: Poetry and the preservation of the soul in corporate America.* New York: Doubleday.

CHAPTER TEN

Earth Connections

There is plenty of evidence (Orr, 1994) that we have become disconnected from the earth and its processes. Each year the ozone layer gets thinner and the amount of ultraviolet radiation increases by approximately 5 per cent. Human corpses now often contain enough toxins and metals to be classified as hazardous waste. Dolphins and whales that wash up on the shores of the St Lawrence River and the Atlantic also contain toxins. The human male sperm count has decreased 50 per cent worldwide since 1938. Industries in the United States release 11.4 billion tons of hazardous waste in a year.

These data reflect a society that builds freeways, shopping malls, and parking lots at a pace that is out of control, where bigger is always better no matter what the cost. Orr (1994) sums up this situation:

> These things are threads of a whole cloth. The fact that we see them as disconnected events or fail to see them at all is, I believe, evidence of a considerable failure that we have yet to acknowledge as an educational failure. It is failure to educate people to think broadly, to perceive systems and patterns and to live as whole persons. (p. 2)

Thus, education has played a major part in the destruction of the earth. Elie Wiesel (1990), referring to education in Germany in the early part of the twentieth century, stated: 'It emphasized theories instead of values, concepts rather than human beings, abstraction rather than consciousness, answers instead of questions, ideology and efficiency rather than conscience' (as cited in Orr, 1994, p. 8). Our education system, with its concern for making citizens globally competitive, is guilty of the same emphases. We still stress cleverness over wisdom in our educational endeavours. Wisdom, or what Orr calls 'true intelligence,' connects information to the broader picture.

Moffett (1994) argues that education should be truly inclusive by situating everything in the largest possible context, which is the cosmos. By constantly locating education within a narrow economic frame of reference, we strip it of ultimate purpose and meaning. Closely related here is what we call career education, where people choose careers based on economic factors. Career choice is thus reduced to some kind of economic model, and, as a result, many people feel alienated from their work and cannot wait until their retirement. Thomas Merton (1985) once called this process 'the mass production of people literally unfit for anything except to take part in an elaborate and completely artificial charade' (p. 11).

Berry, Clark, Dunn, and Lonegran (1991) argue that we are heading into a new period which they call the ecozoic era. The present industrial era they call the cenozoic. Driven by advertising and consumerism, people are invited to take part in what Berry et al. call the 'Wonderworld,' where, even if we have the means to consume these goods, we find ourselves living in 'Wasteworld.' Due to industrialization, competitiveness, and consumerism, we are no longer able to feel or sense the world around us. Berry et al. comment:

> We are not even seeing what we are looking at. We are not even smelling the odors that are around us. Our senses are becoming deadened. Such diminishment of our sensitivities kills off our religious sensitivities and diminishes our understanding. It dulls our imagination. I sometimes say, 'Don't go to sleep, stay awake, stay awake!' (p. 95)

In 1837 the American writer and philosopher Ralph Waldo Emerson began his first book, *Nature*, by expressing a concern that we can share today. He felt that people could not see the world around them and said, 'Why should not we enjoy an original relation to the universe? ... The sun shines today also. There is more wool and flax in the field' (1966, p. 27). If Emerson felt that his fellow citizens had lost an original relation to the universe, what would he think of today's society, where consumerism, the media, technology, and industrialization have deadened our relationship to the natural world?

Earth connections, then, can reawaken us to the natural processes of life. The wind, the sun, the trees, and the grass can help us come alive and waken us from the treadmill we find ourselves on.

Environmental Education (David Orr)

Environmental education has become a part of the school curriculum. Unfortunately, in many cases it has focused on a problem-solving approach to the environment that says we can fix things through recycling or other technical solutions. What is needed is an environmental education that centres on how we are deeply embedded in the natural processes of the earth. It should also give students experiences with these processes. In this part of the chapter I rely heavily on the work of David Orr (1992, 1994), who outlines six principles for rethinking education.

The first principle is that 'all education is environmental education' (Orr, 1994, p. 12). This argument is similar to Moffett's (1994) in that all education must be part of an inclusive context. We need to connect everything to its ultimate reference point, which is the universe itself. Anything less is simply not education.

The second principle is that the goal of education should be mastery of one's person and not mastery of subject matter. Subjects should be seen as means, not as an end, in this process of learning.

The third principle is that knowledge carries with it a responsibility to use it. Many environmental disasters – for example, Chernobyl and Love Canal nuclear accidents – were a result of technology that grew out of control. Orr claims that many of our projects have simply gotten too big, or beyond human scale.

The fourth principle is that knowledge must be looked at from an inclusive context and how it impacts on communities. Orr argues that our economic models never include social and economic costs, and the result is a society on the verge of collapse with excessive violence, terrorist bombings, broken families, and unacceptable levels of unemployment and poverty.

The fifth principle is the need for authentic examples. Orr (1994) suggests: 'What is desperately needed are (a) faculty and administrators who provide role models of integrity, care, and thoughtfulness and (b) institutions capable of embodying ideals wholly and completely in all of their operations' (p. 14).

The last principle is that how we learn is as important as what we learn. For example, lecture courses induce passivity. Too much testing forces students to be receptacles of information rather than individuals who initiate their own forms of learning.

Orr believes that we should educate for ecological literacy. This means that students would be able to see the connections that are inherent in the environment. They would study the basic laws of ecology and how these impact on our day-to-day lives. It would also involve a study of how we got ourselves into the present mess. This would involve a critical look at history and how industrialization and consumerism have contributed to the destruction of the planet. More importantly, ecological literacy focuses on how we can begin to reverse this process. For example, this could mean examining energy accounting and sustainable economies (Daly & Cobb, 1990). Students can also look at a long tradition of sustainable living that includes studying such people as Thoreau, Muir, Gandhi, Schweitzer, Mumford, Rachel Carson, E.F. Schumacher, and Wendell Berry. This tradition involves simplicity, decentralization of power, democratic processes, a sense of place, and human-scale technologies. Orr also states that this tradition is 'dedicated to the search for patterns, unity, connections between people of all ages, races, nationalities, and generations, and between people and the natural world. This is a tradition grounded in the belief that life is sacred' (pp. 94–5).

At a more practical level, Orr argues for a sense of place. In other words, students should learn about the place in which they live. Studying their own place would mean dealing with some of the following questions:

1. What soil series are you standing on?
2. When was the last time a fire burned your area?
3. Name five native edible plants in your region and their seasons of availability.
4. From what direction do winter storms generally come in your region?
5. Where does your garbage go?
6. How long is the growing season where you live?
7. Name five grasses in your area. Are any of them native?
8. Name five resident and five migratory birds in your area.
9. What primary geological event or processes influenced the land from where you live?
10. What species have become extinct in your area?
11. What are the major plant associations in your region? (*Co-Evolution Quarterly*, 1981–2, p. 1)

Gardening

The most important aspect of environmental education is for students to have actual experiences with the earth. One example of this type of learning is gardening. Kiefer and Kemple (1998) in their book *Digging Deeper* describe how youth gardens can be integrated with schools and communities:

> Growing gardens with children is a living testament to how to restore our ancient ties to the natural rhythms of the earth itself. It is in the learning of this lesson – flower by flower, child by child, season by season – that we will be able to reclaim the heritage that is rightfully ours: as the caretakers of a natural paradise where all species thrive. (p. xiii)

Kiefer and Kemple argue that growing a garden has several benefits for children:

- seeing the results of growing food with their own hands
- working in harmony with the forces of nature
- learning basic academic skills in science, math, language, and social studies
- learning to work cooperatively with others

The book is part of the Garden in Every School campaign that began in 1995 and has spread throughout North America. The process not only involves schools and children but includes 'elders to share their experience, stories and practical wisdom; local historians, naturalists, farmers, artisans and other professionals willing to contribute their expertise' (p. xiv) as well as parents and families. To begin the project the school performs a needs survey that looks at such questions as:

- What sites are available for a garden?
- Are there sources of funding?
- What organizations can assist?
- Are there already projects for young people in the community that involve gardening?

This survey can be done formally through questionnaires or informally through phone calls. After the needs survey, an organizing meeting is called. Kiefer and Kemple give detailed directions of how to organize such a meeting. Their book is also filled with case studies for each phase of the process. For example, they describe how San Antonio, Texas, developed a program to become the 'Youth Garden Capital of America.' In that project young people are introduced to different types of gardens such as the 'Brains and Grains Garden,' the 'Dietcise Garden,' and the 'Melting Pot Garden.'

The next phase in the garden-building process is to develop a team. There should be an 'all-weather team,' a core group that does the basic planning and work, and a 'fair-weather team' that contributes to specific aspects of the project. The book is filled with practical information such as an hour-by-hour sample day in the garden and a day-by-day week. They suggest weekly themes that can be used in the garden. For example, one sample theme is soil, in which students examine how soil nurtures the plants in the garden. The case study for this phase is Philadelphia, where Kiefer and Kemple describe how a project called The Village of Arts and Humanities reclaimed parts of the city that had been abandoned and established eight community parks and gardens.

In the third phase the authors identify several possible ideas for garden design. A few of the ideas include the *nutrition garden* and the *heritage garden*, which is based on approaches that have been used in the community over several generations.

In the next phase the garden is brought to life. This phase includes identifying the appropriate site, tilling the soil, laying out the garden, and planting the garden. The authors describe how a composter can be built. The book even deals with issues of class and race, as some African-American families wonder why their children are doing work that was often a burden to their ancestors:

> We know quite a lot about how to value cultural differences and how to heal traumatic wounds. Although the garden has many negative associations, both with past evils and with current values, it also has the potential to heal some of those wounds ...The garden can be a place where self-respect grows, and students who may not do well in the classroom can have a new chance in a different context. The garden can be a haven where no one is ever shamed. Everyone can slow down. (p. 41)

The authors suggest having an opening day ceremony when the ground is first broken. Once the process is started students can keep a garden journal where they describe the plant growth as well as the weeds and insects that also inhabit the garden. Over the summer activities include watering, weeding, and mulching. In the fall, of course, harvesting takes place. Students can save seeds for planting next spring, make edible jewellery, as well as take part in canning, cooking, and freezing the vegetables.

Finally, Kiefer and Kemple suggest extensive procedures for ongoing *assessment* of the project and then for a more summative *evaluation*. They include checklists and sample portfolio contents. Some of the items in the portfolio include student products, student affective surveys, anecdotal observations and reflections, participation graphs, community impact scrapbooks, and culminating activity surveys.

Environmentally Oriented Schools

The rest of this chapter explores how different schools have attempted to approach environmental education. I discuss three examples. First is a public elementary school I visited in Japan, Ojiya School. Second is a private secondary school, Petrolia School, in California. Finally, I discuss the Outdoor School, which provides to sixth graders from different school systems in Oregon an opportunity to learn about their environment in an outdoor setting.

Ojiya School

Ojiya School is a large elementary school near Nagaoka, a city in western Japan. Most of my description of the school is based on Ikue Tezuka's (1994) book. In many ways this is a typical Japanese elementary school, but what distinguishes it is its focus on the relationship to the natural world. When you visit the school, you are immediately struck by the large number of animals. In North America our schools may have one animal (e.g., a gerbil) in the classroom. In contrast, Ojiya is like a little farm with goats, rabbits, chickens, and turtles. Most of the time the animals inhabit an area called 'Friendship Pasture,' where they are fed. The children like to go to the pasture to touch, hold, talk to, and take care of the animals. The children love to hold the animals, particularly the rabbits. When I was there, three children sat on a bench, each holding a rabbit in his or her lap. However, they also have the responsibility of cleaning up after the animals. With so many animals, this is an important responsibility.

Also important to the school is a cluster of trees at the back of the school lot called 'Yasho Homeland Forest.' Before the forest was planted, students surveyed the surrounding area and identified ninety-six types of trees and shrubs that were native to the area. After identifying the different types, the students, with the help of teachers and parents, planted 290 trees in an area of approximately 120 square metres.

When planting the trees, the students considered the distribution of tall and short trees and the colours of the buds, flowers, and fruit. Tezuka (1994) comments:

> The result is beautiful to see. Spring is the season of the biggest change. Many of the trees burst forth in buds and blossoms at the same time. In May, the green grows deeper, and the red blossoms are brilliant against the green background. The red azaleas are especially beautiful. From early summer to autumn, the various trees flower one after another with their white, red, and purple flowers. In autumn the trees bend toward the earth under their load of delicious fruit. Then comes the season of autumnal coloring. (p. 8)

The children love watching these changes. They also like to talk to the trees and write poems. Below are some poems written by children in the third grade:

Trees in The Home Forest
Yukari Kazama

I saw trees in the ground.
They are moving as if they were dancing with snow.
Don't they feel heavy
When they have snow on their branches?

Big Red Buds
Rie Nagahashi

Big red buds on a small tree.
They look like candle lights, red candies, cherries, rubies
Big, red, pretty buds.
Nice buds.
They seem to say, 'I'm pretty.' (pp. 9–10)

At Ojiya School students develop a bond with the animals and the trees so that they do not see themselves as separate from the environment.

Teaching and learning in the classroom also focus on the environment. Tezuka (1994) describes a grade 4 science class where the students are studying caterpillars. The class begins with the students becoming caterpillars as they roll around on the carpet. They also sing the 'caterpillar's song' that they composed as they sway and twist to the music. After this activity they observe the caterpillars and how they move. They also see the eggs change into larvae and then butterflies. Eventually, students developed a play on caterpillars, and one student reported on her experience:

The Day I Became a Caterpillar
Tomoyuki Kanenaga

We made a play about the caterpillars we had studied, and I was to be the caterpillar. On the day of the Festival, I tried to be calm and turn my mind into a caterpillar. But I was very nervous and I thought: 'How can I get over this tension and nervous feeling?' Then I remembered what our teacher said: 'Think sincerely about what we have learned about caterpillars.' Then suddenly I began to see green color before my eyes and I felt as if I were in a cabbage field. (p. 14)

Much of what has happened at Ojiya School is based on the work of Giichiro Yamanouchi, a former principal who is now retired. He has always believed in an integrated approach to learning. In his own words:

Subjects in our present school systems are divided up into small parts. For example, science classes may included observation of fish and rice. But just overseeing them is not interesting or meaningful. Thus, in integrated activity, we connect the curriculum to carp raising and we say, 'Let's raise carp as good as your fathers do!' Then they will be excited and eager to learn about science ... The main contribution we, as teachers, can make to children's learning is to make them excited and impressed with something. Such integrated experiences provide a base for comprehending science, arithmetic, language, etc. (p. 36)

Parents also became convinced of the value of the forest project. Their enthusiasm prompted them to help raise money for the forest. In all the schools where he has served as principal, Yamanouchi worked with parents and community members to help the school. One of his schools was located in a community where raising carp was a local industry. He was able to persuade a person who raised the expensive fish to donate some to the school. The children again learned how to take care of these fish, and the donation of the fish created a lot of community interest in the school. Yamancouchi's work is an excellent example of the subject–community connection discussed in Chapter 8.

Yamanouchi is one of the most interesting and passionate educators I have ever met. Although he is retired now, he is still very active and extremely energetic. Recently he won an award for his work and a day was held in his honour in June 2004. My wife and I attended this day, where former students and parents commented on the impact of having a small forest on the school grounds. One parent got up and talked about how an experience with his daughter at the school had a profound impact on him. One day he went with her to school to look at the tree she was taking care of. There was a small vine growing around the bottom of the tree and the father started to remove it. His daughter got upset and said: 'Don't do that! The vine and the tree are friends.' The father said that his daughter's words strongly affected him, and since that moment he has looked on the natural world in a different way. He said he is much more sensitive to the environment in his work in the construction industry.

Tezuka, in concluding her book, comments on Yamanouchi's work: 'Through the work of such dedicated people as Giichiro Yamanouchi, amazing things are beginning to happen ... There is developing a ground swell movement toward holistic student-centered education in our country' (p. 88).

The Petrolia School

The Petrolia School (Smith, 1995) is a small, private secondary school in rural northern California that has fourteen day students and eight boarding students. The school's main building is a large barn that includes a kitchen, library, basketball court, and gallery. The barn is where most classes take place. Near the barn are three cabins where students and staff live. Simplicity is the rule at the school. The only areas in the barn that are heated are the kitchen and sitting room. All energy used is created on the site. In the summer the energy comes mostly from solar panels that deposit energy in the solar batteries in the barn. In the winter energy comes from a Pelton wheel that is driven by flowing water and that sustains a small hydroelectric generator. The generator provides enough power for the lights, computers, and some music from the sound system.

The school's commitment to site-based energy was tested during a California drought. Instead of accepting the donation of a gas-powered generator, the school burned wood for heat and used a small propane tank to fuel the kitchen stove.

The school, which was founded in 1983, focuses on three goals: academic excellence, environmentalism, and conflict resolution. David Simpson, a former teacher at the school, has had a strong impact on its development. He taught the core course in the school and focused on natural systems and agriculture. The course began with studying world geography and then narrowed down to North America and the local region. In examining the local region, the students would study biology, geology, meteorology, and chemistry. Simpson would then introduce the students to the history of the area and the effect of different peoples on the region, including indigenous residents and the white settlers with their ranching and logging. Students also participated in restoration work and helped plant more than 20,000 trees. Smith comments:

> The work was wet and miserable but fulfilling. A large mural in the kitchen of the school depicts a group of tree planters on a steep slope and serves as a testament to the value people at the school continue to place on linking ideals with practical action. (p. 47)

Although Simpson no longer teaches at the school, his work still influences what happens there. For example, his work as a playwright and theatre producer led to the production of a play called *Queen Salmon* during 1993 and 1994. The play was shown on the west coast to educate people about environmental issues. Smith describes the play:

> Its spirit is well represented in a scene where a human therapist consults a dysfunctional spotted owl family. She tells them that they will simply have to transcend their need for old-growth forests. A companion scene includes the same therapist, now consulting a dysfunctional logging family and sharing the same message with them ... By mixing a strong political message with song and dance and laughter, the play has served to bridge the differences among people and to help them see their shared responsibility for the health of the watersheds in which they live. (pp. 47–8)

Perhaps what is most important about the school is the environmental ethic that permeates the ongoing life of the school. Because of the limited energy supply, if a student uses too much energy listening to the stereo, this can effect others' use of electricity. Gradually, most students learn to balance their individual needs with the community needs.

The school is also run democratically. Students and staff participate in Town Meetings, which discuss critical issues facing the school. Students were involved in the decision, cited earlier, in not accepting the gas-run generator during the drought. Living close to natural systems and trying to live according to an environmental ethic is what Petrolia School is all about. According to Smith:

> Students at the Petrolia School live in a setting where the impact of the land and the weather and other species is unavoidable and where they are in constant contact with adults who have taken as their calling the restoration of natural systems. By bringing students closer to the reality of the natural world, the teachers and supporters of this school are doing much to induct the young into a perspective about place and purpose very different from what is encountered in most contemporary educational institutions. It is this perspective and some of the cultural practices derived from it that may have important lessons for other educators concerned with nurturing an environmental ethic capable of altering the assumptions and expectations that govern so much of life in modern industrial societies. (p. 48)

The school has a website at www.petroliaschool.org.

The Outdoor School

The Outdoor School is different from the Ojiya and Petrolia schools in that it serves eleven school districts in Multnomah County, Oregon. Students from schools in these districts come to the Outdoor School for a period of six days to learn about the environment. Approximately 6,500 grade 6 students and 1,400 high school students, who act as counsellors, come to the Outdoor School, which includes five sites. Besides the counsellors, the staff includes specialists knowledgeable about the environment, six adult counsellors, grade 6 teachers, a nurse, and the cooking staff. Many of the high school student counsellors are students who went to the Outdoor School in sixth grade.

Before students go to the Outdoor School they prepare for several weeks in their own classes. Williams (1992) comments:

> With tremendous excitement, many of the students began to devour the curriculum materials that were to become part of their classroom discovery and discourse. They learned about four major natural resources – animals,

water, soil, plants – presented to them as the *amazing animals, the world of water, the earth beneath us,* and *plants for life.* The students began to realize that they needed to comprehend the ecosystem that they were to inhabit shortly; thus they surveyed and read maps, learned facts related to the four resources, discussed ecological concepts such as *habitat, adaptation, human influence, homeostasis, diversity, community* among others, sketched, labeled, asked many questions, and were engaged in a world of curiosity and wonder as environmental science brought vitality to the classroom. The process seemed to provide credence to Green's (1971) argument that the roots of motivation were to be discovered in one's capacity to wonder. (p. 37)

When they arrive at the school, the students spend a lot of time on a piece of land called the 'study plot,' which is several acres in size. The counsellors take the students around to see the various forms of vegetation such as the ferns, moss, and wildflowers. The counsellors ask questions such as 'Why do you think this twig is bent this way? Why are these creatures crawling away from us?' (p. 39). The counsellors try to let students see the interdependence of the plants, animals, and the environment. They also teach 'environmental manners' so that the students gradually learn to respect their surroundings. For example, one counsellor pointed out to students that if they jump on a decaying log they could kill many of the insects that live there.

The Outdoor School has certain important events or rituals. For example, the last event is a 'soil ceremony,' when trees are planted. As the students surround the tree, they share stories and memories about their six days there. Williams (1992) comments:

And as a further expression of reverence to nature, the community of students and staff stood in silence, many with tears in their eyes, as a tree was planted – the epitome of an ethereal connection. 'I return to the ground its original music,' wrote Wendell Berry in a relevant poem, *Planting Trees* (Berry, 1984, p. 155). The finale of the Outdoor School presented a fitting expression for the renewal of the Earth. (p. 40)

Updated information about the school can be found on its website: www.mesd.k12.or.us/os/index.htm

Environmental Literature

Not all classrooms have the same access to the outdoors as the schools described above. Instead, they can focus on the environment of the school itself. Plants and animals can be brought to the school for the students to take care of. Gradually, they can begin to see the school itself as an environment that needs to be taken care of. Helpful to this process is literature, which awakens our reverence for the environment. Indigenous people's literature is helpful here. I particularly like a book entitled *Touch the Earth* (McLuhan, 1972). For example, below are the words of Walking Buffalo, a Stoney Indian:

> Hills are always more beautiful than stone buildings, you know. Living in a city is an artificial existence. Lots of people hardly ever feel real soil under their feet, see plants grow except in flower pots, or get far enough beyond the street light to catch the enchantment of a night sky studded with stars. When people live far from scenes of the Great Spirit's making, it's easy for them to forget his laws.
>
> We saw the great Spirit's work in almost everything: sun, moon, trees, wind, and mountains. Sometimes we approached him through these things. Was that so bad? I think we have a true belief in the supreme being, a stronger faith than that of most whites who have called us pagans ... Indians living close to nature and nature's ruler are not living in darkness.
>
> Did you know that trees talk? Well they do. They talk to each other, and they'll talk to you if you listen. Trouble is, white people don't listen. They never learned to listen to the Indians so I don't suppose they'll listen to other voices in nature. But I have learned a lot from trees: sometimes about the weather, sometimes about animals, sometimes about the Great Spirit. (p. 23)

Another helpful book is *Earth Prayers* (Roberts & Amidon, 1991), which contains the following Ojibway prayer:

> Grandfather,
> Look at our brokenness.
>
> We know that in all creation
> Only the human family
> Has strayed from the Sacred Way.
>
> We know that we are the ones
> Who are divided

And we are the ones
Who must come back together
To walk in the Sacred Way.

Grandfather,
Sacred One,
Teach us love, compassion, and honor
That we may heal the earth
And heal each other. (p. 95)

Conclusion

In working with Earth Connections our aim is to instill what Albert Schweitzer (1969) called 'reverence for life.' We gradually awaken to the sacredness of all things. We begin to see the earth and its habitants with a new sense of joy and delight. For the very young children, we simple foster and stimulate their natural sense of wonder; for older students and ourselves, we reawaken the sense of awe that we have tended to lose in our mechanistic world.

References

Berry, T., Clark, T., Dunn, S., & Lonegran, A. (1991). *Befriending the Earth: A theology of reconciliation between humans and the earth*. Mystic, CN: Twenty-third Publications.

Berry, W. (1984). *Collected poems*. San Francisco: North Point.

Co-Evolution Quarterly (1981–2, Winter), *32*, 1.

Daly, H., & Cobb, J. (1990). *For the common good*. Boston: Beacon Press.

Emerson, R.W. (1966). *Emerson on education: Selections*. (H.M. Jones, Ed.). New York: Teachers College Press, Columbia University.

Green, T.F. (1971). *The activities of teaching*. New York: McGraw-Hill.

Kiefer, J., & Kemple, M. (1998). *Digging deeper: Integrating youth gardens into schools and communities*. Montpelier, VT: Foodworks.

McLuhan, T.C. (1972). *Touch the earth: A self-portrait of Indian existence*. New York: Pocket Books .

Merton, T. (1985). *Love and living*. New York: Harcourt Brace Jovanovich.

Moffett, J. (1994). *The universal schoolhouse: Spiritual awakening through education*. San Francisco: Jossey-Bass.

Orr, D.W. (1992). *Ecological literacy: Education and the transition to a postmodern world.* Albany: State University of New York Press.

Orr, D.W. (1994). *Earth in mind: On education, environment and the human prospect.* Washington, DC: Island Press.

Roberts, E., & Amidon, E. (1991). *Earth prayers from around the world, 365 prayers, poems, and invocations for honoring the Earth.* New York: Harper Collins.

Schweitzer, A. (1969). *Reverence for life.* New York: Harper and Row.

Smith, G.A. (1995, Spring). The Petrolia School: Teaching and Learning in Place. *Holistic Education Review, 8*(1), 44–53.

Tezuka, I. (1994). *The forest and meadow School.* (D. Bethel, Ed.). Kyoto: Unpublished translation.

Wiesel, E. (1990). Remarks before the Global Forum. Moscow.

Williams, D.R. (1992). The outdoor school: Reverence and connectedness. *Holistic Education Review, 5*(3), 36–40.

CHAPTER ELEVEN

Soul Connections

In defining the holistic curriculum I have stressed connections and relationships as the main vehicle for realizing the student's true nature. This is in keeping with Steiner's (1976) suggestion that 'moving from one thing to another in a way that connects one thing with another is more beneficial than anything else for the development of spirit and soul and even body' (p. 173). It is also possible to directly connect students with their inner lives, or their souls. The soul is defined here as a vital and mysterious energy that gives meaning and purpose to one's life. In my book *Education and the Soul* (2000) I have described my understanding of soul and how it can be nurtured in students, our schools, and ourselves. One element that can help in this process is a *curriculum for the inner life*, as well as the study of world religions and the universe story. Many of the approaches discussed with the other connections can also nurture soul (for example, earth connections, community connections).

Curriculum for the Inner Life

There are a number of ways to stimulate and nourish the inner life of the student. I believe that with TV and videos there is less opportunity for today's children to use their imaginations than in the past. When I was growing up I remember going to my room and listening to the radio sometimes with the lights turned out. As the program unfolded, I would create pictures in my mind.

Storytelling

Before the radio, people would sit around the hearth or campfire and tell stories. These stories would also call on our imaginations. Story-telling can be a powerful way of nurturing soul and connecting with students. Frank McCourt (2005) told personal stories to connect with his high school students. In the beginning he told stories to survive in the classroom. He writes: 'Instead of teaching, I told stories. Anything to keep them quiet and in their seats ... My life saved my life' (p. 19–20). He told stories of growing up in Ireland, such as the following story about his math teacher Mr O'Halloran:

> He'd say, Boys, you have every right to be proud of your ancestors. Long before the Greeks, even the Egyptians, your forefathers in this lovely land could capture the rays of the sun in the heart of winter and direct them to dark inner chambers for a few golden moments. They knew the ways of the heavenly bodies and that took them beyond algebra, beyond calculus, beyond, boys, oh, beyond beyond. (p. 21)

McCourt's text is a wonderful book about how teachers can use stories to connect with students in some of the most challenging situations.

Teachers with younger children have told them nursery rhymes and fairytales. Storytelling is an art, and teachers need to practise the story using their own language and mannerisms and developing their own style. You might first practise telling a story to a friend or partner before using it in the classroom.

Meditation/Centring Practice

The use of imagery and visualization discussed in Chapter 6 is one way to nurture the inner life of students. Meditation is not used as frequently as visualization but some teachers use it in the curriculum. Meditation involves a quieting and focusing of the mind. When we quiet and focus the mind we move to a more receptive mode of consciousness – the listening, intuitive mind. The listening mind is characterized by a still, concentrated awareness. In contrast, in the active mode of conscious-ness the mind is continually chattering, planning, and manipulating. Some teachers prefer to use the term 'centring practice' because of the way some people react to the term meditation.

It is possible to approach meditation from a number of levels. At one level some people use meditation as a vehicle to deal with stress. There is plenty of evidence that meditation practice can lead to lower blood pressure, slower rate of breathing, and a general slowing of metabolic processes (Benson, 1976). The most likely reason for this slowdown is that during meditation practice the individual focuses on one aspect of awareness (e.g., the breath), while during the normal day consciousness is shifting from one stimulus to another countless times. For example, at home, where I am supposed to be relaxing after a long day, I can be reading the newspaper, watching the TV, and talking to my wife at the same time. In meditation we settle down for a while as we simply focus on our breathing. Below are two breath meditations that could be used with students:

> Sit comfortably in an upright position. You can sit in a chair or on a cushion; however, you should keep your back fairly erect. Close your eyes. Now begin to notice the flow of the breath coming in and out of the nose. This meditation involves counting the breaths to yourself as you exhale. You inhale, and then count one as you exhale. Inhale, and count two. You do this up to ten and begin over. Don't worry if you lose track of the counting. Simply return to one and start over.

> Sit comfortably in an upright position and close your eyes. Now focus on the flow of the breath out of the nostrils. As you inhale, mentally note 'in,' and as you exhale mentally note 'out.' If sensations arise, such as an itch, note the sensation and return to the breath. You will have thoughts, so again be mindful of the thought and then return to the breath. Do not try to shut out thoughts; merely be aware of them as they arise in your mind.

In using meditation with students, keep things simple. Meditation is most easily integrated into health and physical education as relaxation exercises. Another meditation is the lovingkindness, or metta, meditation. In this meditation we focus on the heart area and attempt to move that heart energy gradually outwards to others. Since 1988 I have used this to start my classes. I say each phrase followed by a few seconds of silence. This meditation builds on the fundamental principle of holism: interconnectedness.

> May I be well, happy and peaceful.
> May all beings in this room be well, happy and peaceful.
> May all beings in this school be well, happy and peaceful.
> May all beings in this neighbourhood be well, happy and peaceful.
> May all beings in this region be well, happy and peaceful.

May all beings in this hemisphere be well, happy and peaceful.
May all beings on this planet be well, happy and peaceful.
May all beings in this universe be well, happy and peaceful.

Although there are challenges to using meditation in public school classrooms, more and more people are beginning to the make the case for meditation in the schools. Iris Murdoch (1992), the renowned English novelist and philosopher, wrote:

The damage done to inner life, to aloneness and quietness, through the imposition of banal or pornographic or violent images by television, is a considerable wound. *Teach meditation in schools.* [italics added] Some understanding of, and taste for exercises in detachment and quietness, the sense of another level, and another place, a larger space, might thus be acquired for life. Simply sitting quietly and calmly can be doing something good; subduing unkind or frenzied thoughts certainly is. Morality as the ability or attempt to be good, rests upon deep areas of sensibility and creative imagination, upon removal from one state of mind to another, upon shift of attachments, upon love and respect for the contingent details of the world. (p. 337)

Gina Levete (1995), associated with the Interlink Trust in England, has written a document entitled 'Presenting the Case for Meditation in Primary and Secondary Schools.' When students are encouraged to sit quietly, they gain access to their inner life and begin to see their own thoughts. Some forms of meditation, such as the lovingkindness meditation, encourage the development of compassion for all beings on the planet. Meditation can nourish the students' souls and their relationship with other forms of life.

One interesting example of the use of meditation comes from a high school math teacher, Naomi Baer (2003). She had a difficult class, so one day she asked her students to sit still for one minute and then she would ring a bell when the minute was completed. She then asked the students to thank each other after the minute was completed. Over time the students began to look forward to the one minute and even did it when the teacher left the room. She began to use the one minute with other classes, and one group asked to do five minutes every day. Some students from other classes would come and join the one-minute practice. Many students and some parents expressed their gratitude for the one minute:

> Last spring as a student handed in his final exam before leaving for the summer, with tears of appreciation in his eyes, he thanked me for the daily minute. He said it meant a lot to him. This year three students from a class next door come daily to join my class for the minute, afterward thanking their buddies before returning to their own classroom. Parents of former students have come up to me in the grocery store to tell me how much their son or daughter appreciated that minute. They thanked me. (p. 21)

In 1988 I started introducing meditation to my graduate students, who are mostly experienced elementary and secondary school teachers. Along with my colleague, Ayako Nozawa, we did a follow-up study (2002) with some of the teachers who had continued practising meditation after the course was over. Although I did not advocate the use of meditation in the schools, several of these teachers introduced it into their classrooms. For example, one teacher who teaches grade 5 and 6 along with grade 8 drama said:

> I've been doing it now since Jack's course, so I've been doing it for three years, with all the kids, especially in drama, the meditation's amazing, and they love it, they ask me now ... They'll come in ... and now my students ask me, 'Can we meditate, we're really hyper.' Or 'Can we meditate before the test?' (Miller & Nozawa, 2002, p. 187)

This teacher has the students focus on their breathing as a way to focus and relax. She has them visualize going to the beach or lying on a cloud. She also integrates visualization with her teaching so that if they are reading a novel in class she will have them imagine some aspect of the story. In studying ancient civilizations she had them close their eyes and see the pyramids and feel sand blowing on their faces. She sees the impact in their art and poetry: 'I mean I've never seen such poetry. Just with more colorful vocabulary. Colorful words, colorful language' (p. 187).

Another teacher at the high school has introduced meditation to more than 1500 students. She teaches in the Catholic system, and in seven years she has never received a complaint from a parent. She explains how she introduces meditation:

I first create a very safe environment in my class, so people feel very comfortable ... And then we get to a point where I'm saying, 'Now there's a different way to pray. Usually, in our tradition, we mean we need to talk to God, or to the Higher Spirit, but sometimes we need to sit and listen ... So this is a form to connect with your spirit' ... And I have my students journal as well. So I ask for journal reflections and they're very powerful. And now word gets around, because people come to my class the first day and say, 'Are we going to meditate today?' (pp. 187–8)

A teacher who works with students training to be teachers has attempted to integrate mindfulness and lovingkindness into his teaching. He says 'I'm encouraging my classes to take joy in the tasks that are not necessarily glamorous ... and the whole loving-kindness notion is that any kind of direction you give is simply a suggestion in a loving way' (p. 187).

Another individual who taught Grades 4 to 8 in the Catholic system also introduced meditation to her students. Like the secondary school teacher, she connected the meditation to prayer. She found that if she missed a day of meditation the students would insist on doing it. She said that the supply teacher who took over her class told the principal that her classes were always very calm:

And I'm not a very calm type of teacher. I'm a very active kind of teacher, and I have everybody doing different things ... .But I'm sure it's meditation, I can't prove it, but I'm sure it's that thing that brings us together. And it connects – you connect on a different level, you know not just the intellectual. But you connect on a spiritual level and when we were like that in our classroom the supply teacher would notice: This is a very calm classroom. (p. 188)

Dreamwork

A graduate student (Quattrocchi, 1995) has written a thesis on how she used dreamwork at the secondary level. She had students keep journals about their dreams over the course of a year. She found that by working with the dreams, the student gained nourishing insights. All the students who participated in her study commented positively about the experience and some indicated that the dreamwork had enhanced their creativity.

Journals

Another part of a curriculum for the inner life involves keeping a journal. Journal writing is already included in the curriculum of many schools. The reading response journal is used in the language classroom as students record their reactions to what they read. It is even used in other subjects such as math as students journal their feelings and thoughts about the subject (Cohen, 2005). Alternatively, students can keep a 'soul journal' in which they explore their deeper thoughts and feelings. Of course this journal is not for public viewing.

World Religions

During adolescence the conscious search for meaning takes hold. I believe that by studying the world religions this search can be stimulated and, perhaps, some answers provided. Some of the traditional themes of such a course have been identified by Myrna Dales (1987):

Some Topics to Be Explored in the 'Themes in World Religions' Course

Introduction – How does one define 'religion'? Does the concept of religion necessarily imply belief in a god or gods? (For example, can Humanism be considered a religion?) Does there seem to be a trend against or toward faith of some kind? Is religion an 'illusion' (Sigmund Freud) or 'the highest reality' (P. Yogananda)? Which beliefs have developed into 'world' religions, and why have they spread?

An Examination of Creation Stories – Examples can be discussed from Ancient Israel, Mesopotamia, Persia, Egypt, Greece, India, Tibet, and China, etc. Which of these creation stories have been retained in religions existing today (e.g., 'Genesis' in the Hebrew *Old Testament*)?

The Significance of Holy Days, Rituals, and Celebrations in Major Religions – The character, ceremonies, and importance of the Hebrew, Muslim, and Hindu New Year, Christmas, and Easter in Christianity, and the birth and enlightenment of the Buddha will be examined.

Conduct and Morality – How does each religion view man's obligations to the Godhead or religious leaders? What rules of conduct must be followed in dealing with one's fellow man, according to the Ten Commandments, Jesus's teachings, the Buddha's Eightfold Path, and the Hindu Code of Man?

Various Religious Viewpoints of Man's True Purpose in Life – Which religion(s) stress the living of a good life on earth, the preparation for a world to come, or an escape from the cycle of rebirth?

Man's Position with Respect to Other Forms of Life – Does man hold dominion over all other earthly creatures (Judeo-Christian tradition)? Is man one with all creation (Taoism, Hinduism, Buddhism)?

Death and Concepts of an After-life – Concepts of heaven, hell, nirvana, resurrections, and reincarnation as they apply to the religions being studied.

Religious Symbols – Are these basically universal (C.G. Jung), or are they unique in each religion? With what connotations do such symbols as the tree, the mountain, the serpent, light, and water appear in Judaism, Christianity, Islam, Hinduism, Buddhism, etc.?

Religious Leaders, Prophets, and Holy Men – The following will be among those whose importance to their religions will be discussed: Abraham, Moses, Isaiah, John the Baptist, Jesus, Mohammed, the Brahmins, Buddha, Loa-tse, and Confucius.

Concepts of the Godhead – In which religions have religious teachers been deified? In which faiths is the Godhead regarded as immanent or transcendent, or both? If God is transcendent, is He seen as a loving father or a stern judge?

Scriptures – Which religions regard their scriptures as divine revelations and which as teachings? The *Old and New Testaments*, the *Koran*, the *Upanishads* (Hinduism), and the *Tripitaka* (Buddhism) will be discussed.

Art and Architecture Inspired by World Religions – Religious paintings and sculptures will be viewed and related to the concepts which engendered them. The significance will be discussed of such structures as Solomon's Temple, various cathedrals, Islamic mosques, and Hindu places of worship.

The Encounters of Religions – Topics will include Islamic and Christian encounters with Hinduism and the changes in Buddhism as it moved into China and Japan.

Conclusions: Emerging Trends in the Field of Religion – Topics include: 'Back to Christ' movements, the revival of old nature religions, Western adaptations of Eastern religions such as the Hare Krishna sect, and explorations of the possibility of a universal religion.

These themes can be explored by reading the sacred texts and visiting religious festivals and services of the various faiths. Dales comments:

> In the fall, we usually attend the celebration for the Hindu mother goddess ... In the spring, the birth of the Buddha service offers a wonderful glimpse into Shin Buddhism. Zen meditation groups have provided speakers who have answered questions before and after services. Mosque visits have given a sense of Muslim worship far more vivid than that obtainable from books. Synagogues and churches have welcomed student groups. (p. 7)

I would supplement Dales's approach with a study of the mystical thread of each faith and how the notion of the soul (see Chapter 3) is articulated within each tradition. The student can see the commonalities of the major faiths, particularly with reference to the idea of connectedness and selflessness. Related to this notion is the idea of spiritual practice, which is essential to nurturing soul. Students can examine and even experiment with various forms of spiritual practice that are fundamental to realizing our true nature. Spiritual practice brings faith into one's daily life in the most immediate and direct way as the seeker meditates, visualizes, or prays, not just on Sunday, but every day or, ideally, every moment, as a vehicle for reminding ourselves who we really are. The notion of spiritual practice, then, makes religion concrete and specific.

Literature

Literature, mythology, and story allow the self to emerge. Jonathan

Cott (1981) argues that children's literature can play an important role in this process:

> In his 'Immortality Ode,' Wordsworth states that 'our birth is but a sleep and a forgetting'; and the older we get, the harder it is for us to wake up. Children's literature – and what is that but tales and rhymes writ and drawn large or small? – helps us to wake up. It brings us back to experiencing our earliest and deepest feelings and truths. It is our link to the past and a path to the future. And in it we find ourselves. (p. xxii)

I agree with Cott when he says that children's literature is a conveyor of 'wisdom and wonder' (p. xxii). Fairytales, myths, and all forms of children's literature from the around the world can help nourish the child's self. We can draw on literature from all over the world. In Africa, for example, the young child is seen as a messenger from the other world. Cott cites Pierre Erny to make his point in a conversation with the African writer Chinua Erny:

> If an 'angel' ... is seen in the child, education takes a very specific direction. It becomes humble; it gives way to revelation of this being who comes to bring eternally young life to the living ... The child brings along with it more than can be given to it. It renews those who welcome it, rejuvenates them, regenerates them. Child care is composed of piety, admiration, freedom, confidence, and gratitude more than authority or a spirit of domination and possessiveness. (as cited in Cott, 1981, p. 189)

As children mature into young adults they need to be challenged with new forms of literature. In *Holistic Learning*, Miller, Cassie, and Drake (1990) discuss how mythology can assist adolescents in their journey. One of my favourite pieces is Dante's *Divine Comedy*, which describes a journey from Hell to Heaven. This journey is really a metaphorical journey from egotism to the highest form of connectedness-love or, in Dante's words, 'the love that moves the sun and the other stars' (as cited in Miller, 1994, p. 37).

A piece of modern literature that I find particularly inspiring is *The Famished Road* by Ben Okri. The ending of this novel, which won the Booker Prize, is one the most powerful holistic visions I have read:

> We can redream this world and make the dream real. Human beings are gods hidden from themselves. My son, our hunger can change the world,

make it better, sweeter ... It is more difficult to love than to die. It is not death that human beings are most afraid of, it is love. The heart is bigger than a mountain. One human life is deeper than the ocean ... The whole of human history is an undiscovered continent deep in our souls. There are dolphins, plants that dream, magic birds inside us. The sky is inside us. The earth is in us ... Listen to the spirit of things. To your own spirit. Follow it. Master it. So long as we are alive, so long as we feel, so long as we love, everything in us is an energy we can use. There is a stillness which makes you travel faster. There is a silence which makes you fly. (1992, pp. 498–9)

The Universe Story

Finally, science can be a means of discovering the self. Brian Swimme and Thomas Berry (1992) make a powerful case for studying the story of the universe from the Big Bang to the present. This story allows us to awaken to the wonder of existence:

Earth seems to be a reality that is developing with the simple aim of celebrating the joy of existence. This can be seen in the coloration of the various plants and animals, in the circling flights of the swallows, as well as the blossoming of the springtime flowers; each of these events required immense creativity over billions of years in order to come forth as Earth. Only now do we begin to understand that this story of the Earth is also the story of the human, as well as the story of every being of the Earth ... The final benefit of this story might be to enable the human community to be present to the larger Earth community in a mutually enhancing manner. (p. 3)

Swimme and Berry suggest that we are moving from a technological age – the *technozoic* era – to an ecological era – the *ecozoic* era. They call for a United Species that would transcend the United Nations. This new organization could be based on the World Charter for Nature passed by the United Nations Assembly in 1982.

Although the Universe Story is based on the observations of science, it also includes the humanities. Swimme and Berry argue that literature, myth, poetry, music, and all the arts can also express much of the mystery and wonder associated with the story of the universe. In addition to the book by Swimme and Berry, videos can be used in classrooms to help students engage the Universe Story. In sum, the Universe Story could provide a powerful organizing theme for the whole curriculum.

References

Baer, N. (2003). Just one minute. *Inquiring Mind: The Semiannual Journal of the Vipassana Community, 20*(1), 21.

Benson, H. (1976). *The relaxation response*. New York: Avon Books.

Calgren, F. (1976). *Education towards freedom*. East Grinstead: Lanthorn Press.

Cohen, R. (2005). Journal writing in mathematics education: Communicating the affective dimensions of mathematics learning. In J.P. Miller, S. Karsten, D. Denton, D. Orr, & I. Colalillo Kates (Eds.), *Holistic learning and spirituality in education* (pp. 145–52). Albany, NY: SUNY Press.

Cott, J. (1981). *Pipers at the gates of dawn*. New York: McGraw-Hill.

Dales, M. (1987, January). The teaching of world religions. *Ethics in Education, 6*, 6–9.

Levete, G. (1995). Presenting the case for meditation in primary and secondary schools. Unpublished manuscript.

McCourt, F. (2005). *Teacher man: A memoir*. New York: Simon and Schuster.

Miller, J.P. (1994). *The contemplative practitioner: Meditation in education and the professions*. Wesport, CT: Bergin & Garvey.

Miller, J. (2000). *Education and the soul: Toward a spiritual curriculum*. Albany, NY: State University of New York Press.

Miller, J., & Nozawa, A. (2002). Meditating teachers: A qualitative study. *Journal of Inservice Education, 28*(1), 179–92.

Miller, J.P., Cassie, J.R.B., & Drake, S.M. (1990). *Holistic learning: A teacher's guide to integrated studies*. Toronto: OISE Press.

Murdoch, I. (1992). *Metaphysics as a guide to morals*. London: Chatto & Windus.

Okri, B. (1992). *The famished road*. London: Vintage Books.

Quattrocchi, M. (1995). *Dreamwork in secondary schools: Its educational value and personal significance*. Doctoral dissertation, University of Toronto.

Steiner, R. (1976). *Practical advice for teacher: Fourteen lectures given at the foundation of the Waldorf School, Stuttgart, from 21 August to 5 September 1919*. London: Rudolf Steiner Press.

Swimme, B., & Berry, T. (1992). *The universe story: From the primordial flaring forth to the ecozoic era: A celebration of the unfolding of the cosmos*. San Francisco: Harper.

CHAPTER TWELVE

Implementing and Evaluating the Holistic Curriculum

The holistic curriculum is rooted in the presence of the teacher. The first part of this chapter explores this critical variable as well as the importance of caring. I also examine how we can approach accountability in the holistic curriculum and conclude by discussing the process of change.

Presence

Teaching involves three basic factors. First is the theory or assumptions underlying a teaching approach. Some researchers have referred to these underlying assumptions and theories as orientations (Eisner & Vallance, 1974; Miller, 1983). Second are the teaching strategies and practices that we employ in the classroom. The final factor is the presence of the teacher. It is this last factor which is often so critical. If we recall the teachers who have had an impact on us, it is often not their teaching techniques that we remember but their 'presence' that somehow touched us.

The Zen Roshi, Shunryu Suzuki, tells a wonderful story about the presence of a teacher (Chadwick, 1999). He was head of a temple in Japan and was looking for a kindergarten teacher for the temple school. He repeatedly tried to convince a woman to take the job but she refused. Finally he said to her, 'You don't have to do anything, just stand there.' When he said that, she accepted the position. He was convinced that her presence alone would make a difference in the lives of the children. Of course, she did not just stand in the classroom, but Suzuki-roshi identified an important element in teaching.

Emerson, in talking to teachers, emphasized the importance of presence in teaching:

By your own act you teach the beholder how to do the practicable. According to the depth from which you draw your life, such is the depth not only of your strenuous effort, but of your manners and presence. The beautiful nature of the world has here blended your happiness with your power ... Consent yourself to be an organ of your highest thought, and lo! suddenly you put all men in your debt, and are the fountain of an energy that goes pulsing on with waves of benefit to the borders of society, to the circumference of things. (as cited in Jones, 1966, p. 227)

Emerson is arguing that our presence as teachers can be developed by drawing from our depth. Meditation and mindfulness, described earlier in this book, are ways in which we can do this. This connection has also been summarized in a Buddhist poem:

> The thought manifests as the word,
> The word manifests as the deed,
> The deed develops into habit,
> And the habit hardens into character.
> So watch the thought
> And its ways with care,
> And let it spring from love
> Born out of respect for all beings.
> (Source unknown).

For us to be fully present there must then be a fundamental awakening to our inner life – our thoughts and images and their connections to other beings. By being aware of how thoughts arise in our consciousness we can sense our connectedness to others. One teacher in my class expressed how mindfulness enhanced her presence:

As a teacher, I have become more aware of my students and their feelings in the class. Instead of rushing through the day's events I take the time to enjoy our day's experiences and opportune moments. The students have commented that I seem happier. I do tend to laugh more and I think it is because I am more aware, alert and 'present,' instead of thinking about what I still need to do. (Miller, 1995, p. 22)

Teacher presence is often ignored in teacher education despite its importance. It is rarely addressed in pre-service or in-service education. I would argue that meditation and mindfulness practices are simple yet powerful ways in which teachers can enhance their presence. By bringing complete attention to their work teachers can be more effective.

Caring

Being present is also conducive to caring; for if we see the connectedness to others then naturally we care for them as well. Noddings (1984) claims that our schools are in a 'crisis of caring' as 'students and teachers are brutally attacked verbally and physically' (1984, p. 181). Again, this crisis reflects the atomization of society and of schools.

How can the teacher care in this crisis? It is not the responsibility of the teacher to engage each student in a deep interpersonal relationship – this is not possible nor even desirable. According to Noddings, 'What I must do is to be totally and nonselectively present to the student – to each student – as he addresses me. The time interval may be brief but the encounter is total' (p. 180). In short, teachers should simply learn to be with students. In being with students, we are fully present. We do not think about what we will be doing after school or even in the next class, but we engage each student directly. Students can sense when we are not with them, and if this sense becomes permanent, a deep alienation can develop between student and teacher.

Teachers can also show caring by relating subject matter to the interests of the student. If the teacher can make connections between subject matter and student interests, the student will often respond by engaging with the subject matter more directly. As Noddings notes, the student 'may respond by free, vigorous, and happy immersion in his own projects' (p. 181). In her book *The Challenge to Care in Schools* Noddings has described a number of ways in which teachers can bring care into classrooms.

Marcia Umland (1984) also talks about how she cares for her kids in an elementary school classroom:

> Teaching in elementary school can be isolating. A teacher can always do badly – just assign things and get the kids to say them back and then make a good presentation when the principal visits the room. When I wanted to spend all that time with those little people in class, I found that the intimacy I had shared with my peers in college in the sixties was carried over into my classroom. I cared about the students and couldn't stand to sit in the teachers' lounge where they were gossiping about their students ...
>
> I get exhausted, but not burned out. Sometimes I'm dropping my dream for a day or two, but most days I'm on, and stunned by the kids. Lately

I've realized that in setting up a classroom at last I've given myself permission to form a society I'd like to live in. (pp. 155–61)

As Umland relates, caring can help transform the classroom into a community.

Accountability

This is clearly the age of accountability in education. One of the central features of No Child Left Behind is testing at every elementary grade level. In California, Governor Schwarzenegger is pushing for a policy that would link teacher salaries to student test scores. Funding and staffing for schools are also linked to scores in some jurisdictions in the United States.

If this is accountability, it is a distorted version. It reduces education to a competition among students to excel on paper-and-pencil tests. In contrast, a holistic perspective can provide a broader and more inspiring approach to accountability. From this perspective the person, or student, is viewed as a whole human being who thinks and feels and whose physical being is also honoured.

This view of accountability operates at several different levels. First of all we are accountable to the whole student who sits or stands before us. He or she is not to be viewed as someone who simply 'performs' a narrow set of skills. Our willingness and desire to be present are important to this process. *Our ability to listen to students is fundamental to assessing where they are and how we can respond to their needs.* To listen completely and fully is a difficult challenge in a culture that values multitasking and speed; yet it is the beginning of being accountable to our students.

Second, we are accountable to the institutions we work in. This means that as much as possible we work with integrity or what Parker Palmer (1998) calls the 'undivided self.' We work and teach from inside out using what Lincoln called 'the friend deep within' as our guide. By doing this we help create schools where people feel affirmed rather than alienated. Institutions that call for this type of accountability are different from the bureaucratic institution that forces people into limited roles. As much as possible, we try to help create a strong sense of community within our schools. Genuine community creates what we might call an *organic accountability*. Because people are communicating with one another in an open and transparent manner, problems regarding student behaviour and performance can be dealt with directly and with a minimum amount of game-playing. Yes, tests do have a role here, particularly from a diagnostic perspective. They can give us an idea of how a student is doing with regard to a specific set of skills and can help create learning strategies that will improve performance.

Next, we are accountable to our communities in which the schools reside. We make an effort to communicate openly with parents and invite them to participate where possible in the life of the school. The concept of the parent and community volunteer is an important one, particularly in the elementary school, where adults can listen to students read or help with basic math skills. Parent and community involvement in the daily activity of the school is a better form of accountability than so-called advisory councils. Parent involvement in the life of the school is congruent with my notion of organic accountability. Organic accountability is interwoven with what is happening each day rather than with some monthly or bimonthly meeting. Parents and community members who are working with students and teachers on a day-to-day basis have a much more complete view of the students than would be found from looking at a set of test scores.

Reeves (2002) has developed what he calls a method of holistic accountability which goes beyond test scores and includes such factors as community collaboration and leadership practices. He outlines a step-by-by step process for how schools and school systems can take a more inclusive approach to accountability.

At a more global level we are accountable to the planet and the cosmos as a whole. To the planet we owe a sense of reverence and respect for the natural processes of the earth and the biosphere. I know of no better example than the work of Yamanouchi, who developed the idea of planting small forests on the school grounds (see Chapter 10). Students and teachers become accountable to the trees for their health and growth. Our continued focus on a narrow range of student skills is part of a larger societal obsession with achievement and competition at the expense of our relationship to the planet.

Emerson (1966) wrote that each person is entitled to an 'original relationship to the universe' (p. 27). This 'original relationship' is another example of organic accountability. It means that each of us has the opportunity to have our own unique and unmediated relationship with the cosmos. Unfortunately, the media and various forms of technology have come between us and the natural processes of the earth. As a result, we have forgotten the simple pleasures of feeling a soft breeze on our faces, listening to the sound of rain on a rooftop, or witnessing the wonder of the first snow of winter. It is our responsibility as teachers to introduce our students to their 'original relationship' to the universe. Michael Lerner (2000) has argued that the first goal of education should be the development of a sense of awe and wonder, and surely this echoes Emerson's idea of an original relationship to the universe.

Nature itself provides its own method of accountability. The interdependence of ecological systems is an ultimate form of accountability, for if we do not respect these systems and the inherent relations within them, life as we know it will be changed forever. As we witness the interdependence of nature we gradually awaken to a holistic perspective that respects relationships and interconnections. From this perspective we develop and support organic accountability. An organic accountability naturally takes the long view. The pressure for short-term results puts needless pressure on our children.

In sum, much of what passes for accountability today is an artificial form, removed from the fundamental rhythms of nature. But by turning to a holistic and ecological perspective we work toward an organic accountability that is rooted in a much more complete and affirming world-view.

Change and the Holistic Principal

How do we bring about the holistic curriculum in schools? Holistic education requires its own approach to change. The first important element here is for the principal to realize that change is inherent in the life of the school. This is self-evident from the fact that students are growing and teachers are going through changes in their personal lives (aging, for example). Teachers come and go in schools. Even more deeply, we know that change is an organic part of life. From a holistic point of view we simply try to be in harmony with this change; this perspective focuses on alignment or atunement. I believe that many approaches to implementation are problematic as we are usually trying to implement something abstract (for example, a model or a curriculum) rather than focusing on aligning ourselves with the basic processes of life itself.

Change is interdependent and dynamic. The more we become attuned to this reality the deeper and more powerful the change that occurs. We are no longer trying to resist or impose something artificial on the students and ourselves; instead, we give something that is life-sustaining and vital. Below I list some principles that are part of an organic approach to change.

1. *Vision is an important catalyst for change.* Vision is not a mission statement but a lived reality. The vision is implicit in the ongoing life of the school and comes from the hearts and minds of the people who work there. The vision includes some view of the whole and how each part relates to that whole. Of course, it is important that the principal shares the vision since she or he is crucial to the actualization of the vision.

2. *Vision is organic.* There is nothing rigid or fixed about the vision as it changes with our understanding of holistic education. Many teachers have told me that their conception of holistic education keeps changing and evolving. Certainly this has been true in my own thinking, and this book is evidence of that fact.

3. *Have a focus, but avoid detailed plans.* A vision is needed but not a detailed plan. Plans end up being contrary to the flow of life and do not allow principals and teachers to be open to the present moment. Of course, it is important to have priorities and focus; but when we go beyond this with lots of fixed roles and details, trouble starts. Our education system is suffering from too many plans, commissions, and task forces. A teacher working from a deep sense of self is worth more than any recommendation from a task force.

4. *Change occurs at the most basic level from inside out (Hunt, 1987); in other words, deep change occurs when it arises from within the teacher's being.* Long-lasting change occurs when we feel a deep congruence with holistic principles and begin to live and teach according to these principles. In short, there has to be some form of inner transformation for holistic education to work. It can never be mandated or imposed. I have seen this happen with hundreds of graduate students I have worked with. The work in the classroom becomes an extension of their life and is often filled with a deep sense of joy and fulfillment.

5. *Accept conflict.* We know from Nature that conflict is inherent in existence. When conflict or disagreement arises we know that people have awakened from their apathy and have started the first stages of learning. Unfortunately, we fear conflict and confrontation. I am not saying that we should attempt to provoke or instigate conflict; but when it arises, do not attempt to avoid or repress it. It is an important element in any change.

6. *Change is not linear.* The school can best be seen as a complex set of interacting relationships. It is important to understand the sets of relationships that exist within a school, as well as how the school is connected to the surrounding community. When we gain some understanding of these connections, we can bring this sensitivity into our awareness as we work with the staff or a group of teachers. For example, how the principal works with staff is an extremely important factor. If the principal has encouraged and modelled collaboration, then the chances are much greater that significant change can occur.

7. *Acknowledge the non-verbal dimension.* I believe that most change occurs not through language but at a non-verbal level. The unspoken has the greatest power to influence the direction of change. For example, the silent example of a principal or group of teachers deeply committed to a holistic vision can do a great deal to create a climate for change. We have become slaves to slogans and jargon. If we begin to acknowledge the importance of space and silence, we awaken to the place from which language arises. When we acknowledge the non-verbal dimension, words take on a deeper meaning. In silence we notice our thoughts and actions and begin to witness their effect on ourselves and others. If change is tied solely to language and models, it is doomed; when it acknowledges the silent dimension, it begins to unfold in powerful and sometimes wondrous ways.

8. *See the school as a living organism, not as factory.* Here I would like to quote Peter Senge (1990):

Many writers on organization have used the metaphor of 'organization as organism' to suggest an entirely different image for organizational control from that of the traditional authoritarian hierarchy. It is the image of local control – countless local decision-making processes that continually respond to changes, so as to maintain healthy conditions for stability and growth. (p. 293)

Holistic education, then, views the school as an organism and change as organic. Instead of seeing the school as a factory where people behave as if they are working on an assembly line, the school can be seen as a complex living organism that is evolving – changing through a sense of purpose, collaboration, and a deep sense of inner direction.

The primary focus in this whole process is the teacher's personal growth. Of course, the curriculum is important, as the second half of this book indicates; but a holistic curriculum in the hands of a transmission-oriented teacher will become a transmission curriculum.

Ideally, the principal or head teacher will have a holistic vision. The principal should support teachers in their efforts to develop and use the holistic curriculum; if not, holistic teachers will function alone or in small, isolated groups. The principal can use teacher learning teams and help establish a cooperative environment among teachers in the school. The principal can do this by caring for the staff as the teacher cares for the students; in other words, the principal is fully present to the teachers. The principal asks the same questions of herself as she asks of the teachers. The principal takes risks and thus encourages risk-taking in teachers; she does this by being open and vulnerable. By being vulnerable, I do not mean the principal is weak, just that she is not afraid.

The holistic principal realizes that change is gradual and organic and thus approaches it from an ecological perspective. This means that interventions are made with an awareness of their possible effects. Narrow, mechanistic approaches to change are avoided because they do not recognize the interdependent nature of things. Thus, if the principal is establishing teacher learning teams she gives thought to the possible effects for each team rather than hurriedly preparing the groupings. She introduces strategies for professional growth that are not too threatening for staff. The principal intuitively senses what each teacher is prepared to do and what opportunities are appropriate for their growth.

The principal has a vision of holistic education and attempts to live out this vision in her actions. If the principal is able to do this to any degree, teacher growth will be facilitated. The deeper the integration between thought and action, the more powerful the effect on teachers. The vision should provide a sense of direction for the school and be open enough so that teachers can share in the vision and contribute to its development.

What might such a vision look like? I thought it would be appropriate to close this book by offering my own:

At this school we care about kids. We care about their academic work and we want them to see the unity of knowledge. In other words, we want to let students see how subjects relate to one another and to the students themselves. In relating subjects we find that the arts, or more generally the artistic sense, can facilitate these connections. We care about how kids think, and, in particular, we try to encourage creative thinking. We want the students to be able to solve problems and use both analytical and intuitive thinking in the process.

We care about the physical development of the student, and we devote part of the curriculum to activities that foster healthy bodies and positive self-image. We hope to connect the students' bodies and minds so that they feel 'at home' with themselves.

We care about how students relate to others and to the community at large. We focus on communication skills, and as the students develop we encourage them to use these skills in a variety of community settings. At the same time we encourage the community to come into the school, particularly artists who can inspire the students' aesthetic sense.

Most of all, we care about the students' being. We realize that the final contribution that they make to this planet will be from the deepest part of their being and not just from the skills we teach them. We can try to foster the spiritual growth of the student by working on ourselves as teachers to become more conscious and caring. By working on ourselves, we hope to foster in our students a deep sense of connectedness within themselves and to other beings on this planet.

References

Chadwick, D. (1999). *Crooked cucumber: The life and Zen teachings of Shunryu Suzuki*. New York: Broadway Books.

Eisner, E., & Vallance, E. (1974). *Conflicting conceptions of curriculum*. Berkeley, CA: McCutcheon.

Emerson, R.W. (1966). *Emerson on education: Selections*. (H.W. Jones, Ed.). New York: Teachers College Press.

Hunt, D. (1987). *Beginning with ourselves*. Toronto: OISE Press.

Lerner, M. (2000). *Spirit matters*. Charlottesville, VA: Hampton Roads.

Miller, J. (1983). *The educational spectrum*. New York: Longman.

Miller, J. (1995). Meditating teachers. *Inquiring Mind, 12*, 19–22.

Noddings, N. (1984). *Caring: A feminine approach to ethics and moral education*. Berkeley, CA: University of California Press.

Palmer, P. (1998). *The courage to teach*. San Francisco, CA: Jossey Bass.

Reeves, D.B. (2002). *Holistic accountability: Serving students, schools and community*. Thousand Oaks, CA: Corwin.

Senge, P.M. (1990). *The fifth discipline: The art and practice of the learning organization*. New York: Doubleday.

Umland, M. (1984). Writing, elementary school. In K. Macrorie (Ed.), *Twenty teachers* (pp. 149–62). New York: Oxford University Press.

Credits

A version of Chapter 2 previously appeared in *Educating for Wisdom and Compassion: Creating Conditions for Timeless Learning* (2006) by John P. Miller published by Corwin Press.

pp. 30–1 From the *Bhagavad Gita: The Song of God* by Swami Prabhavanda and Christopher Isherwood (cited in *Vedanta* by C. Johnson, © 1971, Vedanta Press).

p. 35 Diagram illustrating Carl Jung's concept of the self, from *Seeing with the Mind's Eye* by Mike Samuels, M.D., and Nancy Samuels, illustrated by Susan Ida Smith, p. 72. © 1975, Random House, Inc.

p. 36 Figure 3.2, 'Our Psyche.' Reprinted by permission of The Putnam Publishing Group/Jeremy P. Tarcher, Inc. from *What We May Be* by Piero Ferrucci. © 1982 by Piero Ferrucci.

p. 38 Material first appeared in J. Miller and Wayne Seller, *Curriculum: Perspectives and Practice* (New York: Longman, 1985). Reprinted with permission of the publisher.

p. 42 From *The Eye of Spirit* by Ken Wilber © 1997. Reprinted by arrangement with Shambhala Publications, Inc., Boston, www. shambhala.com.

p. 44 Distinction between Super-Ego and Transpersonal Self from *The Inward Arc*, 2nd ed. © 1995 by Frances Vaughan. Reprinted by permission of the author.

p. 52 Figure 4.1. Reprinted with the permission of Simon and Schuster Adult Publishing Group, from *The Turning Point* by Fritjof Capra. © 1982 by Fritjof Capra.

p. 56 Extracts from R. Critchfield, *Villages* © 1983. Reprinted by permission of Anchor Press/Bantam Doubleday and Co.

p. 96 Extract from *The Natural Mind* by Andrew Weil. © 1972 by Andrew Weil. Reprinted by permission of Houghton Mifflin.

p. 99 Reprinted from *The Journal of Creative Behavior, 16*(1) (1982): 12, by permission of the publisher, Creative Education Foundation, Buffalo, NY. © 1982.

p. 104 Figure 6.2. Reprinted with the permission of Scribner, an imprint of Simon & Schuster Adult Publishing Group, from *Teaching for the Two-Sided Mind* by Linda VerLee Williams. © 1983 by Linda VerLee Williams.

p. 141 Extracts from Rudolf Steiner, *Practical Advice to Teachers*. Reprinted by permission of Rudolf Steiner Press.

pp. 175–6 Ojibway Prayer from *Earth Prayers from around the World* © 1991 by Elizabeth Roberts and Elias Amidon, published by HarperCollins Publishers. Quoted material is in the public domain.

pp. 184–6 From *Ethics in Education* 6(3)(January 1987): 8.

Index